ILLUSTRATED
ENCYCLOPEDIA OF
HOUSEPLANTS

ILLUSTRATED ENCYCLOPEDIA OF

HOUSEPLANTS

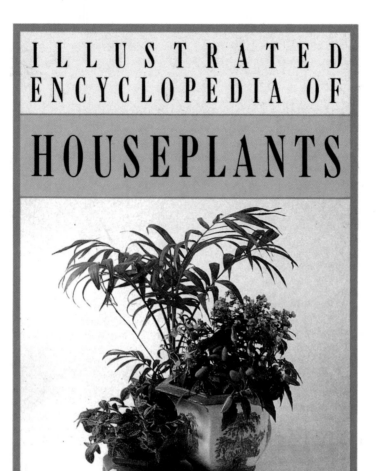

Anna Skalická and Rudolf Šubík

CHARTWELL
BOOKS, INC.

Text by Dr Anna Skalická
Photographs by Rudolf Šubík
Translated by Olga and Ivan Kuthan
Graphic design by Antonín Chmel
Line drawings by Jan Mašek

Published by
CHARTWELL BOOKS, INC.
A Division of BOOK SALES, INC.
110 Enterprise Avenue
Secaucus, New Jersey 07094

Produced by The Promotional Reprint
Company Limited, 1993.

ISBN 1 55521 883 0
Printed in Slovakia by Neografia, Martin
3/11/09/51-03

CONTENTS

DECORATIVE PLANTS IN THE HOME

Decorative plants have become an almost routine addition to the home, providing city dwellers, in particular, with a bit of natural beauty. Bringing greenery into their homes helps to compensate for the absence of wild flowers and plants in a built-up area. People choose plants according to their own individual tastes, provide them with the necessary care, and delight in their blossoms or fruits. So house plants fulfil one purpose—the aesthetic—that is of prime importance to Man. However, plants have other important effects. They increase the oxygen in the air, capture and reduce the amount of dust in the atmosphere, and through the process of transpiration, act as humidifiers. Because their electric charge is opposite to that of Man, they also counteract the effects of static electricity. Furthermore, many plants secrete substances that destroy a variety of micro-organisms, thereby making the atmosphere healthier. Finally, the aromatic substances or essential oils produced by some plants, such as eucalyptus and conifers, are beneficial to people with respiratory problems.

The history of house plants

Growing decorative house plants has a history that goes far back into the past. The ancient inhabitants of Mesopotamia—the Hittites, Assyrians and Babylonians—grew flowers for healing, for use in religious rituals and also for decoration. Ancient Egyptian wall paintings and the remains of plants found in tombs provide evidence of their flower cult. Plants accompanied men to their graves so that they could enjoy them even in the afterlife. Besides making animal sacrifices to the gods, the ancients also burned ornamental plants, especially fragrant woods. The ancient Greeks and Romans, renowned for their admiration of beauty, decorated both their homes and temples with flowers. Animals offered as sacrifice were adorned with flowers to please the gods. The Roman deities included the goddess Flora, in whose honour a festival was held in Rome each spring. To this day, flowers and plants remain important decorative objects in Japan and China, and the traditional art of arranging them in beautiful designs continues to be popular. In Japan, Bonsai are handed down from one generation to the next and are even given as imperial gifts.

The first cultivated house plants were of local origin, but with global exploration and commercial expansion, these were soon augmented by foreign species. The choice of plants has always been determined by the conditions of the home in which they are grown. Consequently, in earlier times, popular house plants were ones that required cool conditions during the winter months. However, in the past few decades, houses have changed quite markedly. Small windows have been replaced by picture windows and patio doors, while central heating has virtually done away with open fireplaces. Modern thermostats can now guarantee a temperature that is both constant and much higher than in the winters of the past. These changes have vastly increased the range of plant species that can be grown indoors and have also made alternative methods of cultivation possible. Besides the traditional method of growing plants in a compost-filled flowerpot, many are now grown in nutrient solutions (hydroponics) which eliminates the need for regular watering and feeding. Easy methods of heating and lighting glass cases make it possible to grow tender tropical plants, moisture-loving Nepenthes or orchids, as well as thermophilous succulents.

Vegetational zones

The commonest house plants, whether grown in living rooms, halls, verandas or conservatories, are usually different species from the native flora and often from a different genus. They are generally plants native to the warmer zones of both hemispheres, primarily the sub-tropical and tropical zones, less often the meridional zone or warm regions of the austral zone. This is because decorative plants of the temperate zone generally have a dormant period in winter when the top parts die back—an unwelcome characteristic in plants grown for room decoration. The exceptions are woody evergreens and perennials that have green foliage even in winter.

Because decorative house plants have their origins in different climatic zones, they also have different cultivation requirements. However, even plants from the same zone may have different requirements. For example, cold-loving plants are found even in the tropics, growing above the tree line at heights over 4,000 m (13,000 ft), in mountainous regions like the Andes. The micro-climates of the individual zones are determined both by the altitude and the moisture conditions (oceanic or continental). The total amount and the distribution of rainfall during the growing season, plus precise ecological conditions including soil type, the amount of sunlight and the nature of the plant community, are distinctive and characteristic for each individual species.

Before they could be grown as house plants on a large scale, these exotic species had to become acclimatized to the changed conditions. Then they generally underwent the process of selective breeding. Acclimatization was the factor that made cultivation possible. Original wild species require far greater care than acclimatized species, so the results would not always be commensurate with the effort of cultivating them. Thanks to selective breeding, there is now a wide range of cultivated forms and hybrids that are relatively easy to grow. These often differ from the original in shape or colour. They may, for example, be small and bushy, have bizarre leaves or double flowers or they may have spotted or variegated foliage. Horticulturalists constantly produce new cultivars and hybrids and so the selection of decorative plants is continually changing and increasing.

ORIGIN OF DECORATIVE PLANTS

At first sight, it may seem surprising that even the most familiar house plants, which often grow side by side, come from such widely different parts of the world. However, it is not so strange when one remembers the changes that the continents underwent in past geological periods. As a result, not only individual species and genera, but even whole plant families, evolved in their own separate ways.

The earth is divided into six floristic regions, unequal in size, but bearing living testimony to this geological history (fig. 1). These six regions are further divided into nine zones (fig. 2). Each zone has its own typical vegetation, primarily determined by the prevailing climate. The two most influential aspects of the climate are temperature and moisture.

The Capetown region in South Africa, although the smallest of the floristic regions, has had an enormous influence on the selection of indoor plants. All species of the family Aizoaceae, some of which, such as the genus Lithops, resemble pebbles in appearance, are from this region. It is home to about 450 species of heaths, and the natural habitat of all pelargoniums, clivias, amaryllises, stapelias, dracaenas, sansevierias and many species of the genus Chlorophytum.

By far the largest number of indoor plants originated in the sub-tropical and tropical zones of two similar but separate floristic regions—the tropics of the Old and New Worlds. These two regions have plants with similar formations and which resemble each other externally. The American cacti and the succulent spurges of the African savannas look similar, for example. Nevertheless, more than half the species that make up the flora of these zones are entirely different. Plant families typical of America

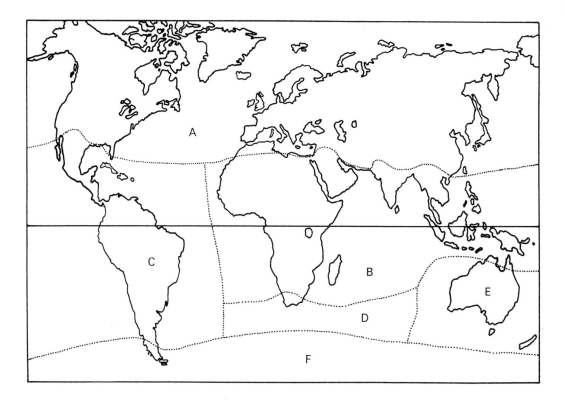

Fig. 1. Floristic regions: A—holarctic region, B—palaeotropical region (includes the tropical zone of the Old World), C—neotropical region (confined to the tropics of Central and South America), D—Cape-town region, E—Australian region, F—antarctic region

include Cactaceae, Agavaceae, Bromeliaceae, Cannaceae and Tropaeolaceae. In addition, many species of the Araceae family, such as the genera Anthurium, Dieffenbachia, Monstera, Philodendron, and the genera Tradescantia, Zebrina, Bougainvillea and Passiflora are characteristic American plants. Typical of the Old World are species of the Nepenthaceae, Musaceae and Pandanaceae families and many genera of the family Orchidaceae. Popular tropical African plants, for example, are species of the genera Saintpaulia, Strelitzia and Ceropegia and tropical Asian genera include Piper, Hoya and Coleus.

Almost all the indoor plants that originated in the holarctic region are from the southernmost vegetational zone, known as the meridional zone, which circumscribes the world. Of course, the requirements of plants from the maritime regions of this zone are quite different from those of plants from the steppe or desert regions in the middle of the continents. Even within the zone, different species and genera are found in the two maritime regions of the Americas (different plants grow on the Pacific coast from those on the Atlantic seaboard), in the Mediterranean region and in the Far East. The meridional zone from the Mediterranean to Central Asia, for instance, is characterized by low summer rainfall. On the other hand, rainfall in the southeast Asian part of the meridional zone is high throughout the year. The most commonly grown house plants from this zone are from the Mediterranean region. They can be transferred outdoors in their containers in summer and do not have to be watered. Typical Mediterranean plants are *Nerium oleander* and *Laurus nobilis*. Plants from the Far East are also popular. These, too, can be transferred outdoors in summer but require regular

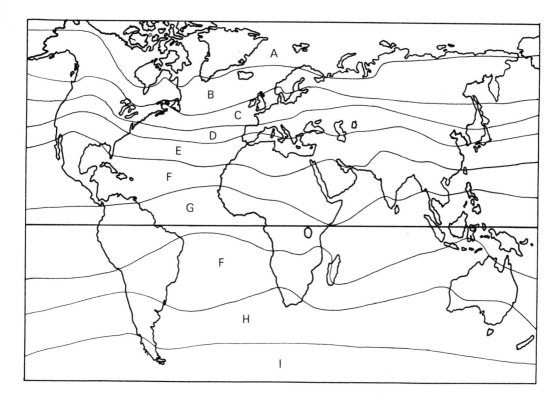

Fig. 2. Vegetational zones: A—arctic, B—boreal, C—temperate, D—submeridional,
E—meridional, F—sub-tropical, G—tropical, H—austral, I—antarctic

watering. Common examples are *Aucuba japonica*, *Fatsia japonica*, *Hoya carnosa* and
Camellia japonica. A great important many of the shrubby evergreen indoor plants are native to
the maritime regions of the meridional zone.

The flora of Australia is distinctive and different from that of the other regions.
Eucalpyti are among the most familiar Australian plants and Callistemons are also
popular and widely cultivated. No decorative plants from the arctic region or from the
cold zones of the holarctic region are grown as house plants. They are only planted
outdoors in parks and gardens.

BASIC REQUIREMENTS OF PLANTS

To grow well, house plants need conditions similar to those of their native habitat.
Generally speaking, all plants require light and moisture and to be kept within a range
of maximum and minimum temperatures. The precise requirements will vary with the
seasons of the year. If the range of these requirements is not observed, the plant dies.
None of these factors acts independently of the other; rather, they are interrelated.
For example, less water is required at lower temperatures because less evaporates
when it is colder. When it is hot, more water evaporates, so more is required.

Seasonal fluctuations in temperature and rainfall are recorded on climate diagrams
of the world. If we know where a plant originally came from, then we can use such climate diagrams to establish its requirements throughout the year. Most house plants

stand up well to British summers and some can even be put out in the garden in their containers. However, they must be taken indoors again well before the onset of frost and wintry weather.

Light and plant growth

No plant, however, finds totally constant conditions throughout the year conducive to good health and good growth. The amount of light is a factor vital to green plants. Light is what controls the biochemical process called photosynthesis. During photosynthesis inorganic substances (carbon dioxide and water) are transformed into organic substances (sugars) by the action of sunlight. These organic substances form the body of the plant and are essential to its basic life functions. So light directly influences the growth and development of plants. During the course of the evolution of different types of plants, the various groups adapted to widely varied light conditions. The ways in which the plant groups adapted depended on the location of their native lands and the character of their habitats, as well as the phases of their life cycles — in other words their periods of rest, flowering, fruiting, etc. So well have plants adapted to different conditions that the diversity of habitats in which all sorts of plant species are able to grow is immense — ranging from the scorching heat of the desert to the deep shade of the herbaceous layer of a rain forest.

A plant's origin, the conditions of the habitat to which it is adapted and the type of situation it occupies in the wild must be kept in mind if it is to be grown successfully in the home. A plant's general appearance serves as a good guide to its individual light requirements. Plants with delicate, pale green to blue-tinged leaves spaced fairly far apart on the stem generally require shade. Plants with stiff, leathery or fleshy leaves and short internodes, often covered with scales or hairs tinged reddish-violet, silvery or dark green, and plants of compact habit, can be put in full sun.

Plants are usually divided into three large groups: those requiring full sunlight, those requiring light of varying intensity but not direct sunlight, and those requiring permanent shade. These groups merely serve as guidelines and there are many plants that come somewhere in between the three without any distinct demarcations. This is particularly true of plants in the second group. Plants in this category include those that require light but not direct sunlight, or else only the slanting rays of morning and evening, those that thrive in diffused light and those that require some degree of partial shade. (Diffused light, for example, is light coming through a rather thick curtain or a thin leafy screen; while partial shade would be found in the undergrowth or indoors away from a window.)

The particular light conditions of any given home can be judged only by the owner himself, but there are a few general rules that can serve as a guide. The corners and walls on either side of a window are the most shaded parts of any room. The light in the corners opposite a window is also poor. The best light conditions are in the window itself. The amount of light passing through the centre of a window to a distance of approximately 150 cm (59 in) represents about 60 per cent of all the light entering a room. The further from the window, the more rapidly the intensity of the light decreases. Much also depends, of course, on the aspect. Windows facing south, southeast or southwest, and to a lesser extent, east or west, provide the most light. Where windows face northwest, northeast or north, the amount of light penetrating the room is much less and the duration and intensity of sunlight is very limited. The intensity of light is similarly influenced by the proximity of trees or neighbouring buildings.

Except for definitely shade-loving plants, such as Selaginellas, and light- and sun-loving plants, such as cacti and bulbs, all species of decorative house plants tolerate diffused light. An easy check for diffused light is that when an object is placed between the plant and the window, it casts a distinct shadow on the plant.

Humidity and moisture

Moisture, both in the soil and the atmosphere, is vital to the life processes of a plant. Plants absorb water through their roots, epidermis and its derivatives (hairs, scales), and return it to the atmosphere by transpiration through the leaves. The absorption and evaporation of water must balance. If the plant has insufficient water, it will wilt. Excessively wet soil, on the other hand, will damage the plant's tissues and it will die.

Soil moisture is provided by watering the plant in accordance with its specific requirements. Again it is important to keep in mind its origin, the conditions of its natural habitat, the temperature of the room and the season of the year. During the growing period, plants generally require more water than during the dormant period.

Atmospheric moisture can be adjusted by syringing and misting, by packing damp moss round the plants, by using humidifiers and by growing the plants in closed, glassed-in spaces. The quality of the water is also important. Hardness, acidity or alkalinity (pH) and the degree of pollution will all affect plants. Plants should never be watered with hard water.

The growing medium

Food is another important influence on a plant's growth. In the wild, green plants obtain food from the soil. Soluble salts, containing what are called biogenic elements, are dissolved in the water absorbed by the plant's roots. Most plants live with their roots anchored in the soil or substrate. Soil is a complex mixture of organic and inorganic substances and is the result of processes taking place in nature over a period of many years. The indoor gardener who wants to simulate a plant's natural conditions must try to provide an alternative growing medium that meets the biological needs of his house plants. Soil requirements differ widely. The types of soils required by plants from a primeval forest, savanna or desert, for example, are very different from those required by marshland or aquatic plants. House plants are generally grown in a blend of soils or soilless composts. Commercial potting mixtures of various types are readily available, or the grower can make his own blend from the components listed below.

Leaf mould is formed by the decay of composted leaves. It is not particularly nourishing and so is only used for growing young plants or for sowing seeds. The quality of leaf mould depends on the type of leaves from which it is made. Beech and oak leaves are best, while horse chestnut leaves are the least suitable. Looseness is an important characteristic of leaf mould. It is added to almost every soil mix at nurseries. Young leaf mould, which is practically unrotted, is used for growing orchids, bromeliads, begonias and ferns.

Rotted turves are obtained by composting turves to which lime and farmyard manure have been added. Pouring liquid manure over them also works well. This is a very nourishing, heavy growing medium with large concentrations of organic substances. It is used in soil mixes for growing chrysanthemums, pelargoniums, petunias and palms.

Frame soil is produced by rotting manure in a frame to which older frame soil has been added. The resulting soil contains up to 25 per cent humus, is a dark colour and is moderately heavy. It is added to a great many mixtures for growing vigorous species noted chiefly for their ornamental foliage.

Composted soil is prepared by composting plant remains to which farmyard manure, lime and loam have been added. After two or three years, this yields a rather light soil, with 10-15 per cent humus and a pH of 7.

Pine-leaf mould is the litter from spruce or pine woods. It is a loose, light soil with a pH of 3.5-5.5 (acid). It dries out rapidly and provides little nourishment. It is suitable in mixtures for many plants that like acid soil, such as azaleas, begonias, sinningias, ferns and heath plants.

Peat is formed primarily by rotting sphagnum moss in an acid environment or by rotting wetland plants on low moors in a rather more neutral environment. It is added to practically all mediums for growing house plants. It improves the soil structure and retains moisture. It is very good for sowing seeds because it is free of micro-organisms.
Loam and peat compost is obtained from peat that is saturated with nutrients and to which heavy loam is added. It is used in almost all mixtures for growing house plants.
Heath mould is another acidic medium. It is formed by the decay of heath plants and is added to soils for growing heaths, azaleas, camellias and similar plants.

Other substances, both natural and artificial, are often added to the growing mediums. Charcoal is one of the natural ones. It is commonly added to the soil mix used for growing epiphytes. Having a large surface area, it absorbs excess moisture and prevents the soil from becoming waterlogged. It also has disinfectant properties, so it is used when propagating plants from cuttings to dust the cut surfaces. Both fresh and dried sphagnum moss have a wide variety of uses. Fresh sphagnum moss is excellent for growing carnivorous plants such as Drosera and Dionaea. It is also regularly used in mixtures for growing orchids, bromeliads and anthuriums. In the case of anthuriums, the top of the soil in the flowerpot is often covered with sphagnum moss to keep it moist. Fern roots are often added to epiphytic mixtures to make them looser. The roots of the Royal Fern, *Osmunda regalis*, and Adder's Fern, *Polypodium vulgare,* are used in this way. The advantage of these particular ferns is that their roots decompose very slowly so that they need replacing only after five to seven years. Crushed pine bark and chopped beech leaves are also frequently added to epiphytic mixtures.

Of the artificial additives, one that is widely used is perlite — andesite expanded at high temperatures. Minute and porous, perlite is excellent for making soil looser. Because it readily absorbs water, along with nutrients dissolved in the water, it is used in propagators. Ceramic granules made from brick-clay are used to aerate the soil. These are commonly used in hydroponics or spread on the surface of dishes for growing succulent plants. Sieved crushed brick is added to compacting soils to lighten them. It is often used by cactus growers. Granulated or crushed polystyrene is similarly used to lighten soil mixtures but it is not water absorbent.

CONTAINERS

Clay flowerpots are the best containers for growing decorative house plants. They are made of unfired clay and are not glazed. As they are porous, the moisture in the soil tends to maintain a balance with the moisture in the atmosphere. However, this is not

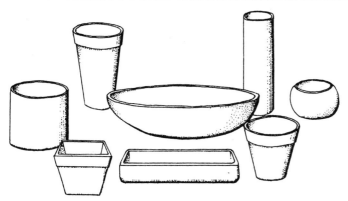

Fig. 3. Various types of containers for growing decorative plants

always advantageous. Plastic pots also retain moisture well. They are cheap, light and modern and practical in design, which makes them suitable for use in arrangements of several plants. In addition, they are available in a wide range of colours to suit any interior decor. Nevertheless, ceramic pots or other ceramic containers continue to be great favourites. They also come in a wide variety of shapes — rounded or angled, flat, shallow or deep (fig. 3).

Container arrangements

Of course, a single species of plant can be grown in a single container, but a combination of several different species grown together is becoming an increasingly popular method. When growing an assortment of plants, however, it is necessary to know the requirements of the individual species. It is impossible to grow desert plants in the same container as moisture-loving ones, or shade-loving species with light-loving ones. Plants also differ widely in their soil requirements. Therefore, plants requiring an acid soil should never be put in the same container as plants that like soil containing lime.

Another important factor in the selection of plants for growing in a single container is their combined aesthetic effect. A combination of plants in harmonizing colours will certainly be more effective than a bland combination of similarly coloured green plants. A striking effect can be achieved, for example, by putting relatively tall plants, such as *Dieffenbachia picta*, its green leaves speckled with cream, in the centre of the bowl, with pendant and prostrate species of Peperomia and Maranta around it.

Pots and flat bowls may also be made more distinctive by putting a moss cone or pillar (fig. 4) in the centre. Take a wooden, plastic or even glass rod, wrap wire mesh or nylon netting round its entire length and then wrap sphagnum or some other moss around that. Hold the moss in place with wire or nylon string. Put some climbing plants in the bowl and anchor them to the pillar as they grow. They will soon root in the moist moss and will rapidly cover the entire surface. Plants that are very suitable for this purpose include *Philodendron scandens*, *Syngonium podophyllum* and *Ficus pumila*. To promote growth, water the moss cone with a weak hydroponic solution.

Hanging containers

Small hanging containers provide a very good method of growing plants in small flats. The containers may be flat on one side, which look attractive against a wall, or spherical and so suitable for hanging in the middle of a room from the ceiling or from a shelf. Many different commercial baskets are available or you can use various plant materials, such as coconut shells or bamboo stalks. The plants grown in the containers should be small, and climbing or trailing species are best of all. These may be put in soil, and some undemanding species may even be grown in just plain water. However, it is best to grow them in a hydroponic solution, for this eliminates the need to water them — which is easily overlooked with a hanging container — and the plants do very well. Plants recommended for such containers are *Hedera helix*, *Ceropegia woodii* and various species of Tradescantia and Rhipsalidopsis.

Fig. 4. Moss pillar

13

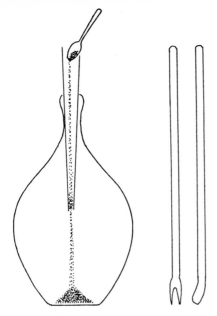

Fig. 5. Demijohn with equipment for inserting plants

Glass containers and bottle gardens

Glass demijohns (fig. 5) and fish bowls (fig. 6 and 7) also take up relatively little space. When properly planted, they are not only very decorative but also extremely suitable for species that require high atmospheric moisture. The only problem is that beginners sometimes have trouble putting plants in a demijohn because of its narrow neck.

First put a drainage layer, such as quartz pebbles, on the bottom and then put in a layer of soil. Pouring soil directly into the neck might dirty the sides, so it is often better to pour it in through a paper funnel extending well below the neck. Insert and tamp down the plants in the soil with the aid of a long spoon of fork. You can make one for this purpose by tying a small spoon firmly to a ruler or a long stick. Tamp the soil down with a cotton reel wedged on a stick.

Some taller plants, such as Syngonium and Calathea, can be grown in a demijohn, as well as low-growing species, such as *Ficus pumila*, *F. sagittata* 'Variegata', Fittonia, Peperomia and Pellionia. Their colourful leaves also make Zebrina and Tradescantia excellent plants for growing in glass containers. Saintpaulias, with their dark blue and purple flowers, are great favourites for planting in fishbowls, together with the attractive leaf rosettes of Cryptanthus. Some Selaginellas that require high atmospheric moisture would normally not last long indoors, but they do admirably in glass containers.

Other glass containers in which house plants can be grown are terrariums and insectariums. These are usually heated and provided with artificial light so that more demanding plants, such as some orchids and bromeliads, can be grown there. A good plant for such containers is *Ficus pumila*, which besides having no special requirements and being easy to grow, quickly covers the walls with green. This small-leaved plant is an excellent foil for Aglaonema and Syngonium species. When selecting plants for the terrarium or insectarium, however, you should keep in mind the kinds of animals that will live there. These might include snakes, lizards, frogs or various insects, and so you should choose the plants accordingly.

Aquatic and marsh plants

Water plants are grown in aquariums. The water hyacinth, *Eichhornia crassipes*, and the water lettuce, *Pistia stratiotes*, both plants that float on the surface, can look very beautiful grown this way.

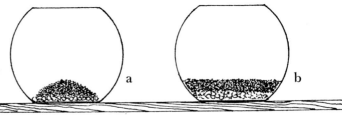

Fig. 6. Glass bowl—incorrectly filled with compost (a), correctly filled with compost (b)

Fig. 7. Glass bowl properly planted

Paludariums offer another possibility for growing plants that are not commonly found indoors. Bog plants (Latin *palus* means marsh) are unusual and not difficult to grow, provided, of course, they are given plenty of moisture. Paludariums are rather large containers and can be made of a variety of materials—ceramic ware, glass, metal or plastic. Suitable plants for the paludarium are *Acorus gramineus, Cyperus alternifolius* and some smaller species of Colocasia.

Epiphytes

Another interesting means of room decoration using plants is growing epiphytes on a branch, stump or piece of tree bark. Epiphytes are plants that grow on other plants without doing the host any harm. They include many orchids and bromeliads, as well as some ferns and aroids. Growing epiphytes in this way requires quite a lot of space if you are going to use a branch or stump. The plants need a suitable environment, artificial lighting in practically all instances and, last but not least, a certain instinct and skill, so they are not ideal for the beginner.

15

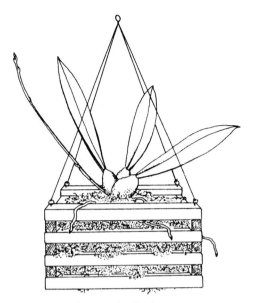

Fig. 8. Hanging wooden basket

The best kind of branch or small stump for growing epiphytes is one with durable wood that is not prone to early decay, especially in a damp environment. The woods of the oak, locust tree, *arbor vitae* and cypress are all particularly suitable. Select an attractively shaped branch or piece of wood. The colour is also important; an interesting or unusual shade can look very effective. The reddish wood of the small trunks found on moors is not only extremely attractive, but also durable, for all the soft parts have long since rotted away. You can also use roots or pieces of bark for growing some epiphytes. You can hang the branch on a wall. In this case, make sure eyes are screwed in firmly and positioned to correspond to hooks fixed to the branch.

If you want a stump to 'be growing' from a dish, then anchor it firmly in the substrate and weight it down with stones. The firmest anchorage is provided by pouring in a little concrete. Keep in mind that water will drip from the plants when they are watered or misted. It is sensible, therefore, to place the dish containing the stump inside another, larger dish or tray to catch all the run off. Prepare a light compost, ideally a mixture of peat, crushed pine bark, polystyrene and fern roots, and put this mixture inside a 'cushion' of sphagnum or other moss, such as Leucobryum, together with the roots of the epiphyte. Then squash the cushion into a compact ball. Wind rustproof wire or nylon line around it and attach it to the branch. A good place for putting plants is in the fork of a branch or in a hole gouged out in advance. Sometimes bits of oak bark can be fixed to the branch to form 'pockets', where plants can be easily held in place.

Maintaining a high level of atmospheric moisture is most important in growing epiphytic plants. This can be achieved by misting with a sprayer, using a commercial humidifier, or by keeping the moss well watered to ensure plenty of evaporation.

A wide variety of suitable plants is available. The funnel-like rosettes of Aechmea, Vriesea and Guzmania are particularly attractive, especially if orchids are grown in between them. Rosettes of narrow, silvery-grey or green leaves are a typical feature of Tillandsias. These usually have no roots and grow without any soil; they may simply be tied or cemented to the branch (the cement, however, must be of a kind that is not water soluble). Special fixatives for air plants are available. Various species of Anthuriums can also be grown on an epiphytic stump. The most suitable ferns are *Asplenium nidus, Polypodium vulgare* and a number of species of Platycerium. The bizarre leaves of Platycerium species create a particularly exotic effect. Popular succulents used for such decoration are Rhipsalidopsis and Ceropegia. If you add a few trailing plants to cover the stump, you will create a truly splendid illusion of the tropics in your home. Plants recommended for this include *Ficus pumila, F. sagittata*, Epipremnum and Syngonium. Where it is possible to provide a higher temperature, *Cissus discolor* is an exceptionally beautiful specimen. The plants need to be watered regularly. Do not let the moss ball dry out completely or it will absorb water very poorly.

Where space is very limited, epiphytes can be grown in wooden baskets (fig. 8) or perforated pots that can be hung from the ceiling, in alcoves or from a shelf. Commonly grown in this way are Platycerium species and some types of orchids.

16

Greenhouse plants

Many plants that are grown in a heated greenhouse may also be grown in a conservatory, glassed-in porch or even a bay window. An extension or bay window forms a sort of glasshouse, although it is open on one side, without any glass separating it from the living room. Of course, this does not provide as much heat and moisture as an enclosed space, but it is still possible to grow some bromeliads and orchids, as well as cacti and other succulent plants here. An enclosed space, such as a lean-to or a miniature conservatory, is separated from the living room by a sliding or removable glass panel or by doors. If artificial lighting is installed it adds a further dimension to a miniature (or full-sized) conservatory, turning it into a delightful decorative feature in the evenings. An enclosed glasshouse of this sort makes it possible to grow plants with demanding heat and moisture requirements. Nepenthes, Guzmania and *Siderasis fuscata* are typical examples.

Large glass-panelled and Wardian cases also serve the same purpose as conservatories. They are like miniature glasshouses but can be placed anywhere inside a room rather than adjacent to a window. They can be located permanently in one position, say between two pieces of furniture, in a corner or in an alcove. Alternatively, smaller cases may be moved to different positions in the room. Plants grown in these sorts of cases must be provided with artificial light—by means of light bulbs along the top of the case. Plant-cases are usually heated electrically.

Hydroponics

All the methods of cultivation of house plants discussed so far are based on the traditional technique of planting them in compost and watering them regularly. Compost is the source of nutrients that, dissolved in water, are taken up by the plants through their roots. After a while, all the nutrients in the compost are used up, so it becomes necessary to give regular applications of feed. Providing a nutrient solution and adequate light are the two major aspects of house plant care (there is always ample carbon dioxide available naturally). Hydroponics—the method of growing plants in a nutrient solution—is based on this simple idea.

The plant is grown in a solution of tried-and-tested composition, which may be regulated by changing the proportions of the individual ingredients. Hydroponics is a 'clean' method of growing plants, eliminating the need for mixtures and fertilizers. At the same time, it decreases the danger of infection from diseases or infestation by pests that may exist in the soil. This method of soilless cultivation is particularly advantageous during prolonged absences from home (holidays, business trips and so on) because there is no need to water the plants.

Two containers are used: an inner and an outer one. Their size depends on the size of the plants. The outer container is a decorative one, but its colours should not be too bright. This contains the nutrient solution. The inner container, which has a perforated bottom, has a physiological function. The plant's roots grow through the holes in the bottom and absorb nutrients from the solution.

Before putting plants in a hydroponic container, wash the roots with lukewarm water to remove all particles of soil. Also, remove all dead roots, taking care not to damage the healthy ones. First fill the container with clean water; rainwater is best. After about two weeks (not sooner) replace this with half-strength nutrient solution. Full-strength solution should only be used once the plants have put out their roots.

Sterile and chemically inert mineral substances are used to support the plants and to ensure that air can reach the roots; these do not provide any nourishment. It is important to use the correct size granules for this purpose. Granules measuring 3-20 mm ($\frac{1}{10}$-$\frac{4}{5}$ in) are a suitable size. Smaller granules render the substrate impermeable to air

and larger ones cause it to dry out quickly. Its chemical reaction must be neutral so that it does not affect the composition of the nutrient solution. It must not be too heavy and the granules must not be sharp or they might damage the plants. For low-growing or trailing plants, a fine and light substrate suffices; for large plants such as Philodendron, Sansevieria, Aglaonema, Dieffenbachia and Ficus, it should have a greater specific weight to ensure the plant's stability. River sand or gravel, clinker, fireclay, perlite and ceramic granules are most commonly used as a substrate.

You can use tap water, rainwater or distilled water. Nutrient salts are then added. A carefully researched formula, in tablet or powder form, is available from most nurseries and garden suppliers. The formula has been worked out so that the salts can be used for all house plants suitable for soilless cultivation. It is important to top up the solution regularly. Plants absorb the water more rapidly than they absorb the nutrients, so, as the solution decreases in volume, it becomes more concentrated. Therefore, it is necessary to add water more frequently than nutrients. Top up the water about once a week in summer and add nutrients every two to three weeks.

Fig. 9. Hydroponic container

REPOTTING, FEEDING AND PROPAGATION

House plants are container grown and so they are inevitably limited in space and, therefore, in the amount of nutrients available. To ensure healthy growth, you must see to it that they obtain sufficient nutrients, which will usually mean repotting from time to time. Plants such as cyclamens, Sinningias and primroses, intended only for temporary decoration, are not repotted. However, plants that you want to keep for a number of years must be repotted regularly.

Use a rather light compost when repotting young plants for the first time because their roots are delicate and cannot tolerate heavy substrates. First of all, cover the drainage hole with a fairly large crock to prevent it from becoming clogged with compost but which will permit excess water to drain away. Then put in a thin layer of coarse sand, small crocks or fine gravel. Cover with a thin layer of potting compost. Carefully remove any dry, shrivelled or rotting roots and then place the plant in the pot. Cover the roots with compost sprinkled round the perimeter of the pot. Press it down with the fingertips. Finally, fill the whole pot with compost to within about 1 cm (½ in) of the rim to allow a little space to prevent spillage when watering the plant.

The best time for repotting most plants is in spring; those that have a definite dormant period should be repotted just before new growth starts. Do not feed plants immediately after repotting. Allow at least two or three weeks for the plants to become established. Then feed in the normal way.

Some plants, particularly those that spread readily and produce long shoots, should not be repotted. Rather, cut off the shoots and immediately insert the cuttings into fresh compost. This is the best method for growing Tradescantia, Zebrina and Scindapsus. Plants grown in a miniature conservatory or plant-case are not usually transplanted and neither are well-developed specimens of Ficus, Monstera, Philodendron and other large plants. It is important, however, that the container is large enough to prevent crowding of the roots. Handling such plants is very difficult. A simpler method than repotting is to remove the top layer of stale compost, replace it with fresh compost and give regular applications of extra feed during the course of the year.

Feeding

Because growing plants deplete the compost of nutrients, these must be replenished by the application of feed. However, over-feeding and erratic application will harm the plants, so it is necessary to observe some rules.

Apply feed only during the growing period, not during the period of rest.

Apply feed only to plants that are well established; not immediately after they have been repotted or when newly propagated.

Use only diluted solution. The proportions should be approximately 1-5 g of nutrient salts per 1 litre of water (0.08-0.2 oz salt per 3½ pt water). Follow the manufacturer's instructions for the rate of dilution and the method of application — on the compost, on the foliage etc.

Regular applications of a small amount of feed of lower concentration is better than a single application of a stronger solution.

See the individual entries on particular plant species for precise details of their feeding requirements.

Feed for decorative plants may be applied in the form of organic or inorganic fertilizers. Organic fertilizers include farmyard manure, cow dung, bird droppings and horn meal. Cow dung is considered to be the best because it is tolerated even by tender plants and is longer-acting. In its dried form, it can be applied directly on to the compost in a ratio of one part cow dung to four parts compost. Fermented liquid cow dung diluted with water — one part cow dung to 10 parts water — can also be used. However, organic manures are rarely used on house plants because some have an unpleasant smell or are difficult to obtain. Inorganic fertilizers are a far more popular choice. These may contain a single nutrient — simple mineral fertilizer — or several nutrients — compound mineral fertilizer.

There are some special rules for feeding cacti and other succulents. It is particularly important to apply feed only during the period of intense growth and flowering. Species that flower in winter should be given applications of feed only at this time. How much and when to feed depends on the particular plant. One or two applications of feed during the growing season are enough for small plants; larger plants should be given greater amounts and fed more frequently. Plants grown in purely mineral substrates should be given regular applications of feed because they obtain no nourishment from any other source. Cacti should be given special cactus feed. This is also suitable for most other succulent plants. Only epiphytic species, such as phyllocacti, should be fed ordinary plant feed.

Feeding orchids is a complicated matter and those who are interested will find detailed information in specialist books. In general, the recommended dosage is a 2 per cent solution of compound fertilizier applied at two-week intervals, alternately on the compost and on the foliage.

Plants of the family Bromeliaceae do not like regular feeding. They should be fed only very occasionally with a weak solution of compound mineral fertilizer. Take care to avoid pouring fertilizer into the leaf rosettes. Organic fertilizers should never be used.

Propagation

Plants can be propagated in two basic ways: sexual reproduction (by seeds or spores) or vegetative reproduction (from cuttings, division, separating plantlets and so on).

Sowing seeds

The size of seeds is the first consideration. Generally speaking, small seeds are sown on the surface, whereas larger seeds are covered with a layer of compost about twice as thick as they are. Press the compost down lightly. Cover the seed tray with a sheet of glass to prevent it drying out. The glass should be turned over at least once a day so that the drops of water which condense on the under-surface do not fall back on the seeds or young seedlings.

A good seed compost can be prepared by mixing sand and peat or well-rotted leaf mould plus some perlite to make it lighter.

Seeds are generally sown in the spring. This allows the young plants to make good growth before autumn and so they are better able to survive the harsh conditions of winter. However, seeds that rapidly lose their germinating power must be sown as soon as they are ripe.

Vegetative propagation

Vegetative propagation is a commoner method for increasing house plants. New plants can be obtained more rapidly and often more simply than from seed. There are several methods, each making use of the characteristic properties of the particular plants. These include plant and root division, taking cuttings from various parts of the plant, and detaching young plantlets or bulbs from the parent plant.

Older plants are often divided when they are repotted. Divide the plants into two or more clumps by gently pulling them apart. If this is not possible, cut them into clumps with a sharp knife. Pot up the separated clumps into suitably sized pots. The 'new' plants continue growth immediately because they have both roots and leaves and therefore do not have to expend energy on forming new ones. This method is used to propagate Clivia, Sansevieria and Aspidistra. Many species of orchids are multiplied by dividing clumps of tubers.

Another very simple method of vegetative propagation is by detaching young plantlets from the parent. Some plants, such as some bromeliads, Ledebouria and *Haemanthus albiflos,* produce numerous offsets. In others, such as *Bryophyllum tubiflorum,* whole new baby plants are formed on the margins of the leaves. *Saxifraga sarmentosa* and *Chlorophytum comosum* produce new plants on long aerial runners, stolons. Small bulblets are often formed on old bulbs and these can be detached. Both young plantlets and bulblets should be potted up immediately into appropriately sized pots and left to root there.

Taking cuttings offers the widest scope for vegetative propagation. Various parts of the plant body, if they are correctly cut off and cultivated, are capable of rooting and growing into new plants. Cuttings of some species will root far more readily than others and some techniques are not suitable for particular plants. For example, cuttings taken from Pelargonium, Tradescantia and Fuchsia root readily and rapidly under normal conditions of growth, whereas those of Ficus, Callistemon and Medinilla root with difficulty and require special handling. Many species, especially grasses

20

and ferns, cannot be propagated by cuttings at all. Success with taking cuttings depends on the ripeness of the plant tissues and on the amount of natural growth hormone present. This is why it is best to take cuttings in spring and early summer.

External factors, such as the rooting medium, micro-climate and growth stimulators, are also decisive. The rooting medium must be loose and rather on the light side. Sometimes only sand is used. It must also be sufficiently moist and warm. Humidity and temperature are crucial. The latter should be about 25 °C (77 °F). The higher the temperature, the greater the need to provide moisture.

A propagator will provide the optimum micro-climate. It may be heated or unheated. A heated propagator consists of a glass or ceramic container with an electric heating element underneath. Alternatively, heat may be provided by placing the container on a radiator. The container is covered with a transparent glass or plastic lid. A plastic bag can make a good do-it-yourself substitute.

Rooting may be stimulated by dipping the cut surface in a proprietary hormone rooting powder. Natural growth hormones present in the cuttings may also be activated by well-considered bruising of the tissues. This can be done by severing the main vascular bundles in the leaf or by making a cut in the stem.

The different kinds of cuttings, depending on the part of the plant from which they are taken, are stem, leaf, root and rhizome cuttings.

Stem cuttings may be herbaceous (soft-stem cuttings) or woody (hard-stem cuttings). They are either taken from the tip of the stem, together with several leaves and buds, or else from a lateral shoot. Usually a long slanting cut is made with a sharp knife. In a few species, such as fuchsias and chrysanthemums, the cuttings are broken off or cut with blunt scissors. As a rule, the cuttings should be put in a prepared rooting medium in a pot and a propagator as soon as they have been taken. Only in a few cases, including pelargoniums and some succulents and spurges, should the cut surface be left to dry before insertion in the rooting medium. The cuttings of many species, particularly Tradescantia, Philodendron, Monstera, sparmannia and oleander, root better in water than in a rooting medium. Put the cutting in a container filled with water and pack cotton wool in the neck to slow down evaporation. Change the water after a week. The remaining part of the cut-off stem of the parent plant often puts out new shoots. Hard cutting back rejuvenates Dieffenbachia, Aglaonema, Ficus and many other plants.

Woody-stemmed plants that are difficult to root, especially Ficus, can be propagated by air-layering. To do this, make an upward cut at a sharp angle beneath a leaf stalk, at the point on the stem where you want new roots to form. Do not cut right through the stem. Carefully insert a matchstick so the cut will not close and brush with hormone rooting powder. Wrap damp moss round the cut and secure with wire. Better still, hold the moss in place with a tube of polythene secured with adhesive tape. This will help to keep the moss moist. Maintain a temperature of about 25 °C (77 °F). Depending on the species of plant, roots will appear at the site of the cut within about three weeks. Cut the stem just below the roots and pot it up, together with the moss packing. The best time for this method of propagation is in June and July.

Leaf cuttings are prepared in one of two ways, depending on the species of plant. The simplest method is to cut off a leaf with a piece of stalk and insert it in a moist rooting medium or in water. Cover the pot with a polythene bag secured with a rubber band. New roots and shoots appear at the base of the stalk. This method is used to propagate Saintpaulia, Cyperus and Peperomia, for example. The leaves of some succulents, such as Crassula, Pachyphytum, Adromischus and Sedum, are broken off and laid on the surface of the rooting medium. Roots and new plantlets grow from the break.

The second method of propagation by leaf cuttings is to sever the main vascular bundles in the leaves or to cut up large leaves into several sections. Insert the sections in the rooting medium with Sansevieria, or merely lay them on the surface with Begonia. Cover with a sheet of glass or a plastic bag.

Root cuttings of such plants as Cordyline and the cuttings from rhizomes of ferns, such as Phlebodium and Cyrtomium, should be left to dry and then inserted in the rooting medium. Each root cutting and section of rhizome must have an adventitious bud which will develop into a new plant.

BOTANICAL NOMENCLATURE

The basic unit of classification of all living organisms, including plants, is the species. The basis for naming all plant species, except mosses and some algae, is the book *Species plantarum* (1753), written by the famous Swedish naturalist Carolus Linnaeus. This was the first consistent use of the system of binomial nomenclature, now recognized internationally. In this system, a plant (or animal) has two names; the first name designates the genus and the second the species.

The scientific nomenclature of plants is governed by precise rules. A plant is given a name and its appearance and characteristics are summed up by an apt description in Latin. The type is designated at the same time. This is the specimen possessing all the distinctive characters of the species used as the basis for comparison with other plants of the same species. Fréquently, plants have been described more than once by different people and given a different name each time; such names are called synonyms (abbreviated 'syn.' in the text).

The names of hybrids may be designated in one of two ways. They may be given the names of the parent species in alphabetical order with an × between the names; for example *Fatsia japonica* × *Hedera helix*. Alternatively, they may have a binomial designation with an × between the generic and specific name; for example, Fuchsia × hybrida. Some hybrids are designated only in the second of the two ways because it is not known which species figured in their parentage; for example Viola × wittrockiana. In the case of intergeneric hybrids an × is placed before the generic name, such as × Fatshedera, which is often formed by joining parts of the generic names of the parents, in this case, Fatsia and Hedera. In some instances species of the same genus are so interbred that they cannot be designated by a specific name. In this case, they are designated by the generic name plus the abbreviation for the word hybrid.

Decisions on the correct nomenclature of plants, not only of species, but of all levels of classification, from the lowest — form, variety, sub-species — to the highest — family, order, class, phylum, kingdom — are determined by the International Code of Botanical Nomenclature. However, the rules are not always observed in practice. For example a later but established synonym may be used as the valid name. There is no book in the world that could contain the 'truly' correct name of plants, for the science of botany is continually developing, evaluations are changed by new discoveries and new species and hybrids continue to be described. Naturally the use of certain names is influenced most by widely circulated handbooks and compendiums. One such source is the *Dictionary of Plant Names* by Encke et al. (1979), which was also used for the unification of the nomenclature in this book.

Cultivars

The names of cultivars are additionally governed by the international code for cultivated plants. Cultivars are designated by the name of the 'botanical' species or hybrid, after which the abbreviation cv. (cultivar) appears. This is followed by the name of the cultivar written with an initial capital letter. Alternatively, the name of the cultivar is written simply in quotation marks.

PLANTS FOR LARGER SPACES

Larger spaces for growing house plants include conservatories, glass-enclosed verandas or balconies, entrance halls and light landings and corridors. An advantage of many modern houses is central heating, which can be regulated to provide a constant temperature both during the daytime and at night.

The plants chosen for larger spaces must be considered carefully and, naturally, must be matched to the conditions of the house. If it is possible to provide higher temperatures, then you can successfully grow cycads, Pandanus and various bromeliads, such as pineapple. Good choices for cooler environments are Sparmannia, Aralia or Araucaria. Lower winter temperatures call for Mediterranean or Australian species. Certain rare and beautiful species of the Proteaceae family or relatively undemanding members of the myrtle family can be used here to good effect. Palms are also very attractive—Howeia, Trachycarpus, Chamaedorea, as well as Phoenix.

Aesthetic considerations are always important. The plants should be suitably arranged for maximum decorative effect. Larger ones should either be placed by the walls or sited as dominant, free-standing specimens—such an arrangement can be very attractive. Walls can also be used for climbing plants.

Grow the plants in pots or larger containers, such as tubs, troughs or bowls. Very occasionally plants can be put directly in open ground in a conservatory (see photograph 1, opposite).

2

3

Acalypha hispida
Euphorbiaceae

Chenille Plant (2). Even though this spurge is widely distributed in all tropical countries, its origin remains unknown. Only two species of this large genus have become popular house plants. *A. hispida* has typical long inflorescences. It is a shrub with large, alternate, ovate leaves, dentate on the margins. The rich, drooping spikes of small reddish flowers may be up to 50 cm (20 in) long. The cultivar 'Alba', with creamy flowers, is also grown, but it is less common.

Cultivation of these decorative plants is not very difficult. They require a light location, but not in direct sun. The minimum summer temperature is 20°C (68°F), and in winter the temperature should not fall below 16°-18°C (61°-64°F). They require high humidity and plenty of water during the growing season. In winter they should be watered sparingly. Do not allow the compost to dry out completely or the plants will shed their leaves. The best method of watering is to spray them with tepid water. The compost must be very nourishing; a good choice is a mixture of peat, leaf mould, frame soil, compost and sand. Repot young plants every year, and older shrubs every two to four years in early spring. If they become too big, the plants may be cut back. Propagate by cuttings at any time of the year. Take stem tip cuttings from the parent plant at the junction between the previous year's wood and the new shoot. Cuttings root very well in a propagator within two weeks.

Acalypha-wilkesiana —hybr.
Euphorbiaceae

Beefsteak Plant (3). Like in *A. hispida* the leaves are large and broadly ovate, and they are variegated with purplish-red as the predominating colour; there are also numerous brownish and greenish blotches. The inconspicuous flowers are arranged in sparse inflorescences in the axils of the leaves, which tend to conceal them. This species is often used for cross-breeding with other species of Acalypha. Cultivation requirements are the same as for *A. hispida* (see above). Note that the more light the plant has, the more variegated are the leaves.

Cycas revoluta
Cycadaceae

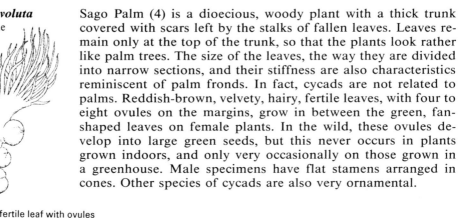

fertile leaf with ovules

Sago Palm (4) is a dioecious, woody plant with a thick trunk covered with scars left by the stalks of fallen leaves. Leaves remain only at the top of the trunk, so that the plants look rather like palm trees. The size of the leaves, the way they are divided into narrow sections, and their stiffness are also characteristics reminiscent of palm fronds. In fact, cycads are not related to palms. Reddish-brown, velvety, hairy, fertile leaves, with four to eight ovules on the margins, grow in between the green, fan-shaped leaves on female plants. In the wild, these ovules develop into large green seeds, but this never occurs in plants grown indoors, and only very occasionally on those grown in a greenhouse. Male specimens have flat stamens arranged in cones. Other species of cycads are also very ornamental.

5

This plant is best grown in a conservatory or a large, glass-enclosed veranda, because the leaves require lots of space. The temperature in summer should be quite high. Cycads thrive in diffused light, as well as in full sun. Water abundantly in the summer, but restrict watering in winter. Feed with organic fertilizer once a month during the growing season, from March till August. Propagate from commercial seed or by detaching the adventitious buds that form on the trunk. The buds will put out roots in moist sand in a propagator.

Nerium oleander
Apocynaceae

Oleander (5). The oleander is mentioned in the works of ancient Roman writers and appears in wall paintings in Pompeii. It is native to the Mediterranean, where it grows beside water courses, often forming large displays. It has decorative, evergreen leaves that are linear-lanceolate and 10-15 cm (4-6 in) long. It bears masses of terminal clusters of pink flowers, although in cultivated varieties these may be white, yellow or red, about 3 cm (1 in) across. Semi-double and double, fragrant and unscented varieties are available. The first flowers appear in June and the last in the autumn.

In order to flower profusely, the plants must be kept in a cool — 4°-10°C (39°-50°F) — and well-ventilated place in winter. Water only when the compost is beginning to dry out.

The plants can be transferred in their containers to the garden, a patio or a balcony in the spring. Take them indoors again before the first frosts. Water abundantly and feed once a week. Oleanders stand up well to pruning, particularly young plants. They are readily propagated by stem tip cuttings that root in water at normal room temperature. The best time for taking cuttings is from June till September. This must be done with care, for oleander is extremely poisonous.

Erythrina crista-galli
Leguminosae

Coral Tree (6) is the name given to this plant in its native land — Brazil. The name refers to the colour of the flowers, which may be more than 5 cm (2 in) long — a rarity in the Leguminosae family. They are arranged in rich inflorescences, sometimes composed of as many as 50 flowers. The calyx is green,

7

Sparmannia africana
—inflorescence

short and bell-shaped; the corolla is leathery. The largest petal, called the standard, curves inwards. The other petals — the wings and keel — enclose the stamens and pistil. The flowers are pollinated by birds. The fruit is a legume. The plant typically has thorny branches and odd-pinnate leaves with thick leathery leaflets. It dies back after flowering and produces new growth in spring.

This woody plant does best in glassed-in entrance halls, verandas or conservatories. It requires abundant light and cool dry conditions in winter. The optimum temperature range is 2°-8°C (36°-46°F). Transfer the plants in their containers to the garden or to a balcony in late May. Propagate by commercial seeds or stem tip cuttings taken in April. Plants grown from cuttings flower sooner than those grown from seed, which may take three to four years. To ensure bushy growth, cut back mature plants in February.

Sparmannia africana
Tiliaceae

African Hemp (7). This South African shrub forms very decorative, hairy, faintly lobed leaves, coloured a striking pale green and up to 19 cm (7 in) long. The white flowers, arranged in thick clusters, have masses of yellow stamens. It is a pity that, nowadays, Sparmannia is a relatively rare house plant because it does poorly in households with central heating, where the conditions are too warm in winter.

Water abundantly during the summer but restrict water in the winter. Sparmannia thrives in plenty of light, but will tolerate slight shade. Feed with compound fertilizer twice weekly during the growing season and once a week during the rest of the year. Keep in a cool place in the winter at a temperature of 7°-10°C (45°-50°F). Repot between spring and autumn after two years. Propagate by stem tip cuttings taken from plants just after their flowers have faded, for then the new young plants will again bear flowers soon. It has a tendency to become leggy and may need propagation.

× *Fatshedera lizei*
Araliaceae

The Ivy Tree (8) was developed in 1910 in the town of Nantes, in France, by the horticultural firm Lizé, hence its specific name. It is a cross between *Fatsia japonica* 'Moseri' and *Hedera helix* 'Hibernica', the Common Ivy. This popular house plant is noted for its evergreen leaves, mostly five-lobed, which are smaller than those of Fatsia but much larger than those of ivy. Only older plants produce flowers and then only rarely.

To grow well, Fatshedera requires cool conditions, about 10°C (50°F) in winter, otherwise the leaves turn yellow. Water freely in summer, but restrict watering in winter. Feed only once a week or once every two weeks during the summer. If you have

8

a garden, transfer the plant outdoors in the summer and plunge it, together with the pot, into the soil. A position in partial shade is best. Propagate by taking tip or lateral stem cuttings in summer. The cuttings should not be woody. Pinch the plants to encourage branching. Cultivation in hydroponic containers has produced very good results. The cultivar 'Variegata' is better suited to modern houses, where the room temperature is usually higher in winter.

Trachycarpus fortunei
Palmae

Chusan Palm (9). This plant is named in honour of the renowned British botanist R. Fortune (1812-80) who, among other things, introduced many plants to Europe. The genus Trachycarpus has only six species. Under suitable conditions the Chusan Palm grows quite tall and is an ideal plant for growing in a large conservatory or glassed-in veranda. The straight trunk is characteristically covered with dead foliage of previous seasons and topped with fan-shaped leaves. The leaf stalks are toothed on the margin and covered with thick fibres on the inner side. This palm is distributed throughout Burma, China and Japan, where it occurs even at high elevations — up to 2,000 m (6,600 ft) — with low temperatures in winter.

10

11

That is why it tolerates low temperatures, even below freezing point, when grown as a cultivated plant. It is one of the hardiest of palms. It does well in a loam and peat substrate mixed with coarse sand which improves the permeability of the medium.

Chamaedorea elegans
Palmae

This palm's (10) generic name is derived from the Greek word *chamai*, meaning low; in fact, it reaches a height of only 2 m (6¹/₂ ft), not only when cultivated as a house plant, but in its

13

native habitat, Mexico, as well. It is usually grown for its foliage, although it also has striking yellow flowers. The leaves are about 1 m (3 ft) long, pinnate and turned slightly downwards. The plant is dioecious and does not produce fruits when grown indoors. However, fruits start to develop rapidly if it is artificially pollinated. There are about 130 other species of Chamaedorea, but these are not grown as house plants.

Chamaedorea does not tolerate direct sun or a dry atmosphere, so mist regularly with tepid water. It thrives at average or higher-than-average temperatures in summer. In winter the temperature must not fall below 12°C (54°F). Feed monthly with a compound fertilizer during the growing period. The soil should never be allowed to dry out completely.

Pandanus veitchii
Pandanaceae

Screw Pine (11). Pandanus has 600 known species, all native to the islands of Polynesia. They mainly grow along the coast, where they form thick stands. Pandanus is an uncommon house

15

16

Sansevieria
trifasciata—rooting of leaf
cuttings

17

Pandanus veitchii—habit
of growth in the wild

plant. Even the most popular *P. veitchii* is seen only rarely in the home. It reaches a height of 2 m (6½ ft) and the leaf rosette measures up to 1.5 m (5 ft) across. The sword-shaped leaves, up to 10 cm (4 in) wide, are striped longitudinally with white and are sharply serrated on the margin. They grow in a spiral on a relatively short stem. Typical of Pandanus are the aerial roots that grow from the stem, become woody and serve as supports for the plant. The inconspicuous flowers are clustered in globose inflorescences but are rarely produced indoors.

Pandanus should be grown in diffused light. It requires high humidity in the summer and should be misted regularly with tepid water; in winter it tolerates a dry atmosphere. Water liberally, until the soil becomes muddy in summer, and moderately in winter. Always use tepid water. Propagate by detaching the young plants that form on the trunk; they root readily in a propagator.

Ficus elastica
Moraceae

Rubber Plant (12, 14). Many species of Ficus are popular house plants because they have such lovely, evergreen leaves. The most widely cultivated is *F. elastica*, characterized by its leathery leaves, glossy on the upper side and dull beneath. When new leaves first appear, they are furled and enclosed by red stipules that fall off as the leaf grows. In its natural habitat in Burma and Malaysia, the Rubber Plant reaches a height of up to 25 m (82 ft). The cultivar 'Variegata' (12) has leaves mottled yellow-white and green. It is particularly well suited to modern houses as it requires higher temperatures in winter, whereas for the type species the temperature in winter should be only about 15°C (59°F). The cultivar 'Decora' (14) differs from the type species in that its leaves are shorter, broader, more leathery, and reddish on the underside, with brownish stipules.

The requirements for indoor cultivation are practically the same for all species of Ficus. The best growing medium is a mixture of frame soil, humus, leaf mould and peat. Water freely in summer when the compost has begun to dry out, but sparingly in winter. The minimum winter temperature is 15°-

18

20°C (59°-68°F). Ficus does not tolerate draughts or abrupt changes in temperature, both of which may cause the leaves to drop. Feed several times a month during the growing period. Repot young plants every year in spring. Large plants need only be repotted if the pot is not large enough for the roots and they become too crowded. Older specimens may drop their leaves, leaving the trunks bare. Cut back to encourage branching growth. Propagation is rather difficult for it takes quite a long time for cuttings to root. The best method is air-layering.

Ficus lyrata
(syn. *F. pandurata*)
Moraceae

Fiddle-leaf Fig (13) has typical broadly obovate leaves that may be up to 60 cm (12 ft) long. This ficus is native to the tropical forests of western Africa. In indoor cultivation it stands up well to central heating. See *F. elastica* for cultivation.

Ficus pumila
(syn. *F. stipulata*)
Moraceae

Creeping Fig (15) occurs as undergrowth in the forests of eastern Asia and Australia. It is a climbing plant which, when grown in a greenhouse or conservatory, may cover windows, walls and even neighbouring plants. It is very attractive on the walls of conservatories or in hanging containers. It is readily identified by the small leaves, which are only 2-3 cm (³/₄-1 in) long, 2 cm (1 in) wide, and crowded on the stem. It requires frequent misting in hot dry conditions to prevent leaf drop. It can be readily propagated by stem cuttings, about 15 of which are put in a 10 cm (4 in) pot filled with a mixture of peat and sand. See *F. elastica* for other cultivation requirements.

Ficus benjamina **'Hawai'** Moraceae	Weeping Fig (16), a species native to India, has become a great hit in recent years. It is most decorative, with its slender, drooping branches and small, long-pointed, leathery leaves, less than 10 cm (4 in) in length. The cultivar 'Hawai' has spotted leaves. Globose fruits, that you would seek in vain on *F. elastica* for instance, often appear, even on young plants. This ficus is well suited for hydroponic cultivation. It is propagated by stem tip cuttings. See *F. elastica* for cultivation requirements.
Sansevieria trifasciata **'Laurentii'** Liliaceae	Mother-in-law's Tongue (17). This plant can be grown with success in a shallow dish and in rather dry conditions. It should be watered only after the compost in the dish has dried out. The leaves of this plant are edged golden-yellow. To produce offspring with the same golden-edged leaves, propagate only by division of the clumps of older plants, not by leaf cuttings; plants grown from cuttings produce green instead of variegated leaves. The inflorescence is shorter than the leaves and composed of fragrant yellowish flowers. The species *S. cylindrica*, which has tube-like leaves with joined margins, is also interesting, but it is grown only occasionally.
Citrus sinensis (syn. *C. aurantium*) Rutaceae	Orange (18) is a small evergreen tree grown in sub-tropical climates and is probably native to southeast Asia; however, it is not known in the wild form. It was probably first cultivated in China, and is now a very popular house plant, particularly

20

21

when it bears flowers and begins to develop fruit. The fruit is a special kind of berry called a hesperidium; the outer layer of the pericarp (flavedo) is coloured orange or yellow and the inside layer (albedo) is white. In the orange, the rind adheres tightly to the pulp and is more difficult to peel than the loose-skinned mandarin orange.

In winter, the orange requires a low temperature of 5°-10°C (41°-50°F); when grown outdoors, it even tolerates a light frost. Water liberally in summer but restrict water in winter, especially if it is grown in cool conditions. It does not tolerate water containing lime. Orange may be propagated by seed sown in spring, or by cuttings, taken with three to five buds any time between spring and autumn. Cuttings produce results more rapidly. The best method of propagation, however, is by grafting on to *Poncirus trifoliata* or *Citrus aurantium* seedlings.

Citrus reticulata
(syn. *C. nobilis*)
Rutaceae

Mandarin (19) is another popular citrus plant grown in the home. The genus Citrus includes at least 60 species; many are the result of spontaneous cross-breeding or of cross-breeding in cultivation, but their origin is often unknown. Characteristic

42

features of the mandarin are small spines and small leaves, only 3.5 cm (1½ in) long, with short, practically unwinged stalks. The flavedo separates readily from the albedo.

However, if you cannot provide very cool conditions in winter — less than 10°C (50°F) — it is better not to try to grow it as a house plant. Limit watering in winter, but water liberally from spring until autumn. The mandarin grows best in a loam and peat substrate with a pH of 4-5.5. Feed the plant once a week during the growing period. In winter feed only at intervals of one to two months. More robust plants may be lightly pruned to the desired shape. Young plants are readily obtained from seed.

22

As a rule, the seeds germinate well and rapidly, but plants grown from seed bear fruits only after many years. If you want the mandarin to bear fruits the best method is grafting.

Bougainvillea spectabilis
Nyctaginaceae

The best known of the 14 species of Bougainvillea are *B. spectabilis* (20) and the smaller *B. glabra*. Most specimens grown indoors are hybrids (designated *B. × buttiana*), of which there are a number of different cultivated varieties, and *B. glabra*. The species illustrated here is a very attractive specimen for the conservatory. This is a liana native to Brazil. The branches are spiny and covered with alternate, hairy leaves. The flowers are

24

small, yellow-green, and relatively inconspicuous. However, the three bracts surrounding the flowers are magnificent. These are usually violet, but may also be red, pink or orange.

To produce flowers bougainvillea must be kept in a light, cool place in winter at a temperature of about 5°-10°C (41°-50°F). It also needs plenty of light during the growing period. Water sparingly in winter, but liberally from spring onwards. Trim the plant to remove straggly growth and promote bushiness. Propagate from lateral stem cuttings.

Ptychosperma macarthuri
Palmae

The genus Ptychosperma includes approximately 15 species, widespread in Australia and some nearby islands. In its native habitat this palm (21) reaches a maximum height of 8 m (26 ft). It often forms several slender stems topped by large pinnate leaves, 150-300 cm (5-10 ft) long and 60-100 cm (23-39 in) wide, with alternate, irregularly tipped leaflets. The leaves curve in an arch from the stem. The fruits are bright red and the seeds are deeply furrowed — hence the scientific name of the genus (*ptyche* = fold, furrow, *sperma* = seed).

The individual species are easy to grow indoors. They tolerate even rather low winter temperatures of 8°-10°C (46°-50°F). They are grown from imported seeds that germinate quite readily. They do not even need higher temperatures for germination. They require heavier composted soil, as do most palm trees.

25

Impatiens walleriana
(syn. *I. holstii,*
I. sultani)
Balsaminaceae

Busy Lizzie (22). The genus Impatiens includes some 600 species. This plant, native to the mountains of tropical Africa, is 30-50 cm (12-20 in) high and very branched. The branches are thick and fleshy with pale green leaves that are pointed-ovated with toothed margins. The lower leaves are alternate, the ones on the upper part of the stem are arranged in whorls. The flowers are usually single, growing from the axils of the leaves. They are about 4 cm (1½ in) across and typically have a spur that is very slender and slightly curved. The colour of the flowers is usually pink, but they may also be white, red or violet.

Water liberally in summer, but in winter water sparingly just to prevent them from drying out. This species does not tolerate direct sun. It is suitable not only as undergrowth to taller plants in large spaces, but also as a potted plant for room decoration. This undemanding plant may be increased from seed, or more simply by stem tip cuttings or lateral shoots that root rapidly at a temperature of 15°-20°C (59°-68°F). After they have rooted, they should be cut back to promote branching.

Hibiscus rosa-sinensis
Malvaceae

This shrub or small tree (23, 24) — 2-5 m (6½-16 ft) high — is easy to prune so that it does not take up too much space indoors. The dark green leaves are glossy on the upper surface and toothed on the margins. The calyx of the large flowers — up to 15 cm (6 in) across — is typically subtended by an epicalyx. The petals are pink, but there are many cultivated forms with carmine-red or yellow flowers. The protruding stamens are very decorative; their filaments are joined to form a column and separate only at the top. There are also many popular double forms (flore pleno — fig. 24). Specimens with spotted leaves (cv. Cooperi) are common, too.

    H. rosa-sinensis is widely grown in the greenhouse and is also a popular indoor plant. It requires abundant light and can tolerate full sun. Provide a rich compost and adequate room in the pot for the roots to grow. Water liberally from spring until autumn and feed with compound fertilizer twice a month. When

schematic diagram
of the flower

26

young the plants should be cut back to obtain bushy growth. Transfer the plants in their pots to the garden or balcony in the summer. The flowers do not last long, but new ones are produced continually so that the plant is never without blooms. Propagate by stem tip cuttings.

Pittosporum tobira 'Variegatum'
Pittosporaceae

P. tobira (25) and *P. undulatum* (with sinuate leaves) are the two most commonly grown of the 160 species of Pittosporum. This relatively rare, sub-tropical woody plant was brought to Europe in 1804 from its native habitat in China and Japan. It is a very bushy shrub with attractive, glossy, leathery leaves which are longish ovate. They are 10-12 cm (4-5 in) long and 3-4 cm (1-1½ in) wide, and coloured deep green spotted with white in the cultivar shown here. The fragrant, yellowish-white flowers are borne at the tips of the twigs, surrounded by clustered leaves. The shrub is attractive even when it bears fruits, for the capsules, leathery at first, later become woody and remain on the plant a long time.

27

28

Cool greenhouse conditions are suitable. Propagate either by stem tip cuttings in late summer or from imported seeds. Sow seeds immediately as they rapidly lose the power to germinate.

Ananas comosus
(syn. *A. sativus*)
Bromeliaceae

The Pineapple (26, 27) is best known for its fruit, and few people know that it is a decorative plant suitable for growing indoors and in the greenhouse. It is native to Brazil, but is grown on plantations throughout the tropics. The wild form is unknown. Plants with leaves striped yellowish-white to pink ('Variegatus', fig. 27) are particularly attractive. When grown indoors, the Pineapple rarely bears flowers and never bears fruits. Even so, the sterile Pineapple is very decorative, with its large rosettes of rigid, spiny-margined leaves, 80-120 cm (31-47 in) long. The small flowers are clustered in dense, globose or ovoid inflorescences.

The fruit is a multiple fruit consisting of yellow berries grown together with the fleshy stem and bracts into one mass. The stem growing through the centre is surmounted by a crown of stiff leaves. This crown can be used to propagate the plant. Cut it off carefully and leave it to dry. After a few days, insert it in sand or in sandy compost. The Pineapple can also be increased by offsets in the same way. To induce flowering in a mature plant, wrap translucent plastic foil round it, including the pot.

49

Put some apples inside; these produce gaseous ethylene which causes bromeliads to put out flowers. Maintain a temperature of 27°C (80°F).

The plants should be grown in diffused light. Water freely in summer and mist with tepid water regularly. It does not matter if water collects in the leaf rosette. Feed occasionally with mineral fertilizer.

Allamanda cathartica
Apocynaceae

Golden Trumpet (28). The genus Allamanda has 12 species, all of them native to South America, and one native to Central America. This plant is native to Brazil. Its name aptly describes the shape and colour of its flowers, which measure 8-12 cm (3-5 in) in diameter. The leathery, glossy, longish ovate leaves, with pointed tips, are 10-14 cm (4-5½ in) long and 3-4 cm (1-1½ in) wide. Arranged in whorls of three or four, the leaves are very decorative. Because this liana reaches a height of 6-8 m (20-26 ft) in the wild, and about 2 m (6½ ft) in the greenhouse, it cannot be grown indoors without repeated pruning. This, however, often prevents flowering.

Golden Trumpet requires full sun, liberal watering and ample space. It may be increased by stem tip cuttings.

Howeia belmoreana
(syn. *Kentia belmoreana*)
Palmae

Kentia Palm (29) is usually grown in corridors, conservatories and large halls. In its native habitat — the islands of the Pacific — it reaches a height of 8 m (26 ft). The stem is thickened at the base and the huge leaves, up to 2 m (6½ ft) long, are deeply cleft all the way to the mid-rib. It differs from the similar species, *H. forsteriana*, which has long-stalked leaves, dotted with scales on the underside and spreading outward horizontally or drooping. Kentia Palm has ascending leaves with very short stalks and without scales on the under-surface. It hardly ever flowers when grown indoors. *H. belmoreana* has been cultivated in Europe since 1858 (first of all in England) and *H. forsteriana* since 1872 (in Belgium).

Araucaria excelsa
(syn. *A. heterophylla*)
Araucariaceae

Norfolk Island Pine (30). Those who like conifers could not choose a lovelier one for home decoration than the Norfolk Island Pine, with branches arranged in regular tiers and fresh green needle-like leaves. This araucaria, like the other 17 species of the genus, is native to the southern hemisphere. It takes its name from the island of its origin. All Araucarias have evergreen, needle-like leaves and large cones that disintegrate when fully developed. *A. bidwillii* of Australia has the largest cones; these may be up to 30 cm (12 in) long and 23 cm (9 in) across.

Norfolk Island Pine is not difficult to grow. It requires rather cool conditions; in winter a temperature of 5°-10°C (41°-50°F), or even less. Water liberally in summer and mist the entire plant regularly. If you have a garden, plunge the plant into the ground in a shaded location in the summer. It does not tolerate direct sun. Repot after two to three years in early spring before new growth starts, but take care not to disturb the root ball.

30

Sometimes removing the top layer of compost and replacing it with fresh compost will suffice. Be sure it does not contain lime. Feed with organic fertilizer only if the plant has not been re-potted for a long time.

Sanchezia nobilis
Acanthaceae

inflorescence

The genus Sanchezia, named after the Spanish botanist Sanchez, includes some 60 species distributed throughout Central and South America. *S. nobilis* (31) began to be cultivated in Ecuador. The leaves are large, up to 30 cm (12 in) long, with prominent yellow stripes along the veins. In this, it is very similar to *Aphelandra squarrosa*. Dense inflorescences of yellow flowers about 5 cm (2 in) long appear at the ends of the stems. The bracts from the axils of which the flowers grow are also decorative; they may be as long as 4 cm (1½ in) and are coloured a vivid red.

  S. nobilis requires warm and moist conditions throughout the year. It grows quite rapidly, so it should be pruned every year; new plants can be grown from the cuttings. After they have become established young plants should also be pruned to induce bushy growth. It does well in sandy frame soil in a rather large container. It grows best in a greenhouse or conservatory. In winter it tolerates direct sun.

Medinilla magnifica
Melastomataceae

Rose Grape (32) has drooping panicles of pink flowers, 30-50 cm (12-20 in) long, with large bracts of the same colour. The distinctive leaves are leathery, about 30 cm (12 in) long, with prominent, curving veins. The strong, quadrangular stems are winged. It is native to the Philippines.

For good growth it requires a light, slightly acid compost, such as a mixture of leaf mould, peat, forest litter and sand. Water liberally, feed weekly and mist daily during the growing season. The temperature should never fall below 15°C (59°F). Water very sparingly in winter. Although it is readily increased from seed, propagation by softwood stem cuttings is a more rapid method. Cuttings may be difficult to root and a propagator is essential.

33

Aloë marlothii
Liliaceae

This (33) is 2-4 m (6½-13 ft) tall, with dense tufts of as many as 50 leaves. These are more than 50 cm (20 in) long, up to 10 cm (4 in) wide at the base, vivid blue-green, and red-toothed on the margin. The inflorescence is branched and composed of glowing yellow flowers.

To produce flowers, *A. marlothii* requires plenty of light, warm conditions in summer, and cool conditions in winter. Water only in very hot weather; do not feed.

Aloë arborescens
Liliaceae

This South African aloë (34) is the most widely grown species of the genus. It was once cultivated for its medicinal properties for treating suppurating wounds. In its native habitat it may reach a height of 3-4 m (10-13 ft), but only 1 m (39 in) when grown indoors. The fleshy leaves are coated with a greyish bloom and are spiny-toothed on the margins. The inflorescence may be up to 80 cm (31 in) high and is composed of drooping flowers coloured a vivid red edged with green.

This plant requires a light, sunny position. Water regularly whenever the compost is beginning to dry out. It should not be fed. It requires cool conditions in winter but the temperature should not fall below 6°C (43°F). It makes numerous offshoots by means of which it can be readily propagated. Stem tip cuttings also root very quickly.

34

CACTI AND OTHER SUCCULENTS

Succulents are plants with some fleshy parts — roots, stems or leaves. This is not an end in itself, but an extraordinarily ingenious adaptation to the environment in which these plants live. The succulent parts serve as reservoirs of water to enable the plants to survive the uncongenial conditions of their natural habitats — arid places exposed to the full heat of the sun and with only occasional rain.

Cacti are all plants of the Cactaceae family. Other succulents belong to a wide variety of different families in which, for example, only the members of a single genus may be succulent; or even just some species of certain genera, such as the commonly grown pelargoniums. Major families of succulents are the Euphorbiaceae, in which some species resemble cacti, Aizoaceae, which include the familiar living stones of the genus Lithops, Asteraceae and Liliaceae.

It is not possible to give general rules for the cultivation of succulents because of their immense range. Therefore, details are given separately in the text accompanying each illustrated species. Cacti, however, are an exception. Although many species are undemanding with no special requirements, they must all be provided with certain basic conditions. First of all they require sun. Those without a sunlit window should not try to grow cacti. A greenhouse, conservatory or miniature conservatory is ideal. The compost should be well permeable, preferably a mixture of rotted leaf mould, frame soil, loam and sand. Cacti grown in an inert medium, such as crushed brick, should be given a regular application of special feed. Water fairly freely in summer (cacti tolerate more moisture than one would think). In winter severely restrict watering or even withhold it altogether. Cacti require a consistent low winter temperature of about 5°-10°C (41°-50°F).

Glasshouse with cacti (35 — opposite)　　　　　　　　　　　　A Mexican desert (36)

36

37

Astrophytum
myriostigma
Cactaceae

Bishop's Cap, Star Cactus (37) is very popular and widely cultivated. Five other species of Astrophytum are also often grown as house plants. The illustrated variety, *tetragona*, has only four ribs. The generic name, which means star-like plant, is derived from Greek and describes the shape of this cactus, with five to eight pronounced ribs that form the stem. At first the body is globose, growing taller later and becoming columnar in age. It is without spines and covered entirely with white, felted spots that prevent the evaporation of water. The form *nuda* does not have felted spots and so its stem is green. Spaced along the edges of the ribs are large woolly areoles without spines. The flowers, which arise in the shallow depression on the crown, are

38

large, 4-6 cm (1½-2¼ in) in diameter, and coloured pale yellow. The filaments, anthers and seven-lobed stigma are also yellow. The seeds are large and brown. Propagate from seed, not by grafting.

Astrophytum asterias
Cactaceae

This species (38) was discovered in Mexico by a Russian aristocrat who sent several specimens to St Petersburg, all of which eventually died. He also sent one specimen to Professor J. Zuccarini, at the University of Munich, who described it as *Echinocactus asterias*. This specimen also died and the species was considered to be extinct. In 1923 the Czech collector A. V. Frič recognized this cactus on a visit to the botanical garden in Mex-

59

ico City. It is considered to be the loveliest species of the Astro-phytum genus. The globose body is absolutely symmetrical, slightly flattened, the crown depressed and covered with brown felt. It is 6 cm (2¼ in) high, about 10-25 cm (4-10 in) across, and coloured grey-green. The slightly rounded ribs are fairly insigni-ficant, with a shallow groove in which grey-felted areoles, 5-10 mm (⅕-⅖ in) across, are spaced. The glossy yellow flowers with carmine throats are 6-7 mm (⅕-³⁄₁₀ in) across. This cactus is easily propagated from seed which germinates readily at a tem-perature of about 25°C (77°F). Like *A. myriostigma*, it requires plenty of light, heat and moisture in summer. In winter, it needs light and a temperature of about 10°C (50°F).

Echinocactus grusonii
Cactaceae

This cactus (39) was introduced into cultivation from Central Mexico. The specific name is in honour of H. Gruson of Magdeburg, owner of a large cactus collection. It is a popular species with cactus growers. The stem is very large and spheri-cal — up to 80 cm (31 in) across and 130 cm (51 in) high. It has about 30 sharp ribs dotted with felt areoles bearing eight to ten straight or slightly curved radial spines up to 3 cm (1 in) long and coloured pale yellow. The four central spines are up to 5 cm (2 in) long. The crown is thickly felted. Golden-yellow flowers about 5 cm (2 in) long and 5 cm (2 in) across are ar-ranged in several rows in a circle on the crown.

Water fairly freely in summer; the compost must never dry out. Water sparingly, but regularly, in winter. It does not tolerate strong sun which might cause sun scorch. Propagate only from seed, which germinates rapidly at a temperature of 25°C (77°F).

41

Aporocactus
flagelliformis
(syn. *Cereus flagelliformis*)
Cactaceae

This species (40) grows naturally on trees and rocks in Mexico. It was brought from America to Europe in the early 18th century (some authors claim it arrived as early as the late 17th century). Its long-standing popularity as a house plant is undoubtedly due to its unusual shape, for it has slender stems about 2 cm (^{3}/$_4$ in) across and up to 1 m (39 in) long. These are longitudinally ribbed with areoles spaced 3-7 mm (^{1}/$_{10}$-^{1}/$_5$ in) apart and terminated by 15-20 reddish-brown spines. In early spring the areoles on two-year-old stems produce zygomorphic flowers, 7-10 cm (3-4 in) long and coloured reddish-violet.

It looks very attractive placed high up on a shelf, cupboard or in a hanging container. It thrives if it is transferred outdoors in May to a balcony or windowbox. Water abundantly in summer. It requires a nourishing compost with an admixture of peat. Repot only infrequently and when essential.

Leptocladonia
microhelia
f. ***microheliopsis***
Cactaceae

The plants (41), which grow singly, not in groups, have a stem that is more or less columnar in age, unribbed, but covered with tubercles arranged in a spiral. There are 30-40 radial spines and six to eight, blackish-brown central spines. The radial spines radiate outwards and so look like small suns (hence the plant's specific name). The flowers are a pale purple colour with golden-yellow throats.

62

Because this plant has a flat root system, like mammillarias, it does best in a flat dish. It requires a mineral free-draining, but nourishing, compost with plenty of sand. Water freely during the growing period. In winter, the most suitable temperature is 5°-10°C (41°-50°F).

Gymnocalycium friedrichii
Cactaceae

This cactus (42) is native to the open forests of Paraguay, where it tolerates the hot and dry climate as well as the periods of heavy rain. *G. friedrichii* and *G. mihanovichii* are two of the most commonly grown species of this genus. It reaches a height of only 5-6 cm (2-2¼ in). The stem has eight sharp ribs coloured brownish-red; in young plants these have pale stripes on the sides and shining skin that looks as if it were wet. The areoles

42

Grafting of cacti

are white and woolly with five long, slightly curved spines. Even young plants have buds covered with naked scales. These develop in early spring and do not finish flowering until autumn. The flowers are pale pink; the fruits are red. The brown seeds are very small.

In Europe, it thrives best in a hotbed or heated greenhouse. Water liberally in summer. In winter it will do without any water for a long time at a temperature of 10°C (50°F). It does not tolerate direct sunlight.

Ferocactus latispinus
Cactaceae

This species (43) is found in abundance on calcareous substrates in Mexico and Guatemala. It is one of 30-35 species forming the genus Ferocactus. The globose stem of old plants may be up to 40 cm (16 in) across. It is coloured blue-green and generally has 20 narrow, sharp ribs, 15-25 mm (^{1}/$_2$-1 in) high. The areoles are grey-felted and carry 8-12 radial spines radiating outwards; the four central spines are arranged in the form of a cross, the lower spine is up to 3.5 cm (1^1/$_4$ in) long and 8 mm (^{3}/$_{10}$ in) wide – hence its popular German name *Teufels-*

43

44

Ferocactus latispinus
—spines

zunge, meaning devil's tongue. This spine is transversely furrowed and downcurved at the tip. All the spines are a pale
reddish colour. The flowers have a very short tube and the
scale-like bracts are broad and bare. The colour of the blossoms
may be white, pink or violet-purple. The ovoid fruits are yellowish to reddish and retain the remnants of the perianth a long
time.

It requires a nourishing compost and plenty of sun and heat.
It grows very slowly and may be propagated only from seed.
Many growers consider ferocacti the loveliest of all cacti.

Mammillaria bocasana This (44) is a popular species of the large genus Mammillaria,
'Rosea' Cactaceae which, apart from Opuntia, includes the gratest number of spe-

65

cies of all the genera in the family Cactaceae. Hundreds have been described to date, but only about 170 can be counted as valid. These are rather small, spherical cacti that make side shoots freely so that older plants form many-headed clumps. The stem measures about 4-5 cm (1½-2 in) and is completely covered with fine, grey-white spines growing from conical tubercles. There are 25-30 very delicate radial spines. A long, central spine, 2 cm (¾ in) long, usually coloured red or brownish, terminates in a hook. The inconspicuous flowers are about 15 mm (³⁄₅ in) long and 10 mm (³⁄₁₀ in) across and coloured pale pink with a central, darker, red stripe on the outer petals. They are always produced in abundance. The more decorative fruits, which may be 3-4 cm (1-1½ in) long, are a vivid red, and remain on the plant for a long time. The seeds are brown and glossy. This cactus is a great favourite with novice growers.

Selenicereus grandiflorus
Cactaceae

Queen of the Night (45) is a snake-like cactus that twines around the trunks of trees in the forests of Central America. The long stems, with numerous aerial roots, are slender, only 2-3 cm (¾-1 in) across. They have five to seven sharp angles. The areoles are white-felted with yellowish spines. The plant takes its name from the magnificent blossoms that open at night. It is a pity that they last such a short time, for they dry up the morning after they open. They may be up to 30 cm (12 in) long and have a relatively long tube covered with scales. The outer petals are orange-yellow, the inner petals pure white. They have a pleasant, vanilla-like fragrance.

Growing this species is not very difficult. It requires adequate heat and a light compost with plenty of humus. The best support for the plant is a bamboo pole. Greenhouse-grown specimens rapidly form stems several metres long. It requires warm conditions in winter.

Rebutia senilis
Cactaceae

This cactus (46) is from northern Argentina. Like most Rebutias, it has a flattened, spherical stem with tubercles arranged in a spiral. The delicate, intertwined spines, numbering about 25, are up to 3 cm (1 in) long. The flowers grow from the lower part of the stem and are 3.5 cm (1²/₅ in) across, quite large in relation to the small size of the plant. They are coloured carmine-red to yellow-red. They last several days, closing in the evening, but opening again in the morning. The tube is narrow and covered with several delicate, scale-like bracts.

It is a very undemanding plant and numerous lovely flowers

46

47

are often produced twice a year — in spring, and a second time in autumn. Because it is naturally a plant of the mountains, it easily tolerates great differences between daytime and night-time temperatures, and between summer and winter temperatures. For good growth, water liberally and provide adequate ventilation. Propagate from seed or by detaching new young plantlets. Because it produces numerous offshoots, new specimens may be obtained in a relatively short time.

Rebutia krainziana
Cactaceae

This species (47) is thought to have originated in Argentina. It was described in 1948 by the distinguished Swiss horticulturist, Kesselring, according to living specimens purportedly brought to Europe by the German collector of cacti, Ritter. It probably no longer exists in the wild. Like *R. senilis*, it produces numerous offshoots, so that it soon forms large groups of flattened, spherical stems about 4 cm (1¹/₂ in) across. They are a matte green and the ribs are formed by small tubercles. The large areoles are white, thickly woolly, with 8-12 short, soft, snow-white spines. In spring the plant bears a profusion of bright red flowers with yellowish throats.

No special care is required to grow it indoors. It will grow in ordinary compost with adequate watering. It should be protected from excessively strong sun by light shading. Crossing with other species of Rebutia has yielded cultivars with white blossoms.

49

Cereus peruvianus 'Monstrosus'
Cactaceae

This species (48) was cultivated as early as 1576, but is no longer to be found in its original habitat. Like all members of the genus Cereus, this plant has a long, columnar stem that may be up to 3 m (10 ft) high in mature specimens. It branches profusely and the young shoots are pale green, later becoming blue-green. The stem usually has five to eight ribs. The areoles are whitish; four to seven radial spines and one or two central spines grow from them. The flowers, which open at night, are pure white and large — about 16 cm (6 in) long. The tube is usually without scales and glabrous.

Various monstrous forms (see picture) are often grown indoors. It grows fairly rapidly and so requires fairly nourishing compost. Water liberally and feed regularly in summer. Propagate from stem segments, as well as from seeds, which have good powers of germination.

Mamillopsis senilis
Cactaceae

This species (49) is native to northern Mexico where it grows in the mountains at elevations of 2,500-3,000 m (8,000-10,000 ft), tolerating both frost and snow. It resembles a snowball with its

70

thick, 'woolly' coat. The stem is spherical at first, later oval in outline, about 4-7 cm (1½-2¾ in) across. The 'woolly' coat is composed of numerous white (sometimes yellowish) radial spines, 40-50 growing from a single areole. The central spines are hooked and brownish-yellow at the tip. The flowers have a very long tube – up to 6 cm (2½ in), are slightly oblique and are coloured orange-red to carmine-red. The ripe fruits are red and globose.

This is an attractive, hardy cactus but it does not produce flowers very often. To induce flowering, keep it in a cold but

50

very light place in winter. The substrate must be free-draining and the plant should be watered with great care during the growing period.

Cephalocereus senilis
Cactaceae

Old Man Cactus (50) is native to Mexico. Because many natural habitats have been destroyed by collectors, its export is prohibited by the Mexican government. The long columnar stem is usually unbranched and, in its native land, this cactus can attain a height of 15 m (49 ft) and a diameter of about 40 cm (16 in). The 20-30, not very high, longitudinal ribs are green at first, later grey. The areoles are rimmed with 20-30 delicate white spines which may be up to 12 cm (5 in) long. The central spines are only 2-5 cm ($^3/_4$-2 in) long. Flowers are produced only by mature plants that have attained a height of about 6 m (20 ft). Coloured pale pink, they are usually 5 cm (2 in) long and 7.5 cm (3 in) across. They emerge from a rufous-brown cephalium — a special formation of clustered areoles, wavy wool and bristles developed on top of the stem, and open at night.

Growing *C. senilis* is relatively easy. Its only requirements are plenty of light and warmth. It is usually propagated from seed, sown in heavy clay compost at a temperature of 10°-15°C (50°-59°F).

Lobivia famatimensis
Cactaceae

This cactus (51) is native to northern Argentina, where it grows in the mountains. It was introduced into cultivation by Kurt Backeberg, the renowned expert on succulents, and soon became a great favourite in cactus collections. The body of this tiny cactus is almost spherical, measuring only 30-35 mm (1¹/₅-1²/₅ in) in height and slightly less in diameter. The crown is flat with a marked depression in the centre. There are 24 longitudinal ribs coloured grey-green. The areoles are white-felted and have six soft spines on either side. The flowers, emerging on the upper third of the stem, are 3.5 cm (1²/₅ in) long, large in relation to the body, and range in colour from white to yellow-orange and red, depending on the variety (the picture shows var. *haematacantha*). The stamens, the style and the stigma are yellow. The fleshy fruits measure about 1-1.5 cm (²/₅-³/₅ in) and are completely covered with pale reddish-brown hairs.

It is easy to grow. Keep it cool and dry in winter. Propagate from the readily produced offshoots, either grown on their own roots or grafted on Cereus stock.

52

Notocactus ottonis
Cactaceae

This species (52) is distributed throughout southern Brazil, Uruguay, Paraguay and Argentina. The illustrated specimen is the cultivar *N. ottonis* f. *vencluyanus*. It differs from the type by having reddish-orange blossoms. Like every other species of this genus, it has a purplish-red stigma. The globose body, 5-11 cm (2-4 in) across, has 6-13 ribs that are not very pronounced. The areoles carry 8-15 radial spines coloured yellow and three to four central spines coloured brown. The flowers, measuring up to 6 cm (2½ in) and coloured a deep vivid yellow, emerge in a wreath round the thickly woolly crown. The fruits are relatively small, retaining the remains of the perianth for a long time. The seeds have short dry appendages (strofioles).

Melocactus matanzanus
Cactaceae

Melocactus (53) is the oldest known genus of cacti in Europe. They were found by Christopher Columbus on the coast of the West Indies, where they still grow. Cuba is the native land of the species shown here; other members of the genus are found in Central and South America. It has a pale green body, about 9 cm (3½ in) across, with eight to nine sharp ribs. The strongly curved spines are white. Typical of every Melocactus is the semi-spherical formation on the crown, called a cephalium,

53

where flowers, and later fruits, develop. The orange-red cephalium makes an interesting contrast to the green of the stem. The body of Melocacti is spherical (the word *melo* means melon), with prominent ribs and long spines. The minute flowers and cylindrical fruits are reminiscent of the genus Mammillaria.

It requires lots of sun in summer. Water freely and mist regularly in summer. Keep dry in winter and ensure that there is adequate light. The optimum winter temperature is about 15°C (59°F).

Melocactus
curvispinus
Cactaceae

This species (54) is one of 60 that have been described to date. These are distributed from Mexico to South America. It has a spherical body with 10-12 prominent ribs. Seven radial spines and two central spines grow from the areoles. The radial spines are 1.5 cm (³/₅ in) long and curved (hence the specific name); the central spines, up to 2.5 cm (1 in) long, are straight. The cephalium appears only after 10 years and the flowers produced there are relatively small. The only other spherical cacti with similar cephalia are of the genus Discocactus, but these have large flowers. Identifying the various species of Melocactus is

56

difficult because young plants differ markedly from older individuals.

Imported species are usually more difficult to grow, but plants propagated from seed do very well. The warm conditions of modern houses are suitable for their growth.

Opuntia ficus-indica
Cactaceae

This cactus (55) is an important food plant, for the large fleshy fruits are eaten by Man and the stems are fed to cattle. It is native to tropical America, but is cultivated throughout the world. It has, for example, become completely acclimatized to the Mediterranean region. Jointed stems, which may be flattened, and which are called pads, are typical of the whole genus Opuntia. It is said to include as many as 470 species and, next to Mammillaria, is the largest genus of cacti.

Opuntia microdasys
Cactaceae

Bunny Ears, Golden Opuntia (56) is a very popular and decorative species, native to Mexico. The stem, reaching a height of 1 m (39 in), is composed of numerous flat, oval pads, 15 cm

57

(6 in) long and 10 cm (4 in) wide. They are coloured emerald green. The areoles, up to 2 mm ($^1/_{10}$ in) across, are yellowish and felted at first, later brownish. The spines (glochids), growing in thick tufts, are very fine and a nuisance when the plant is being repotted because they catch in the skin. Wear leather gloves when repotting, as the glochids might cause inflammation of the skin. The flowers, measuring nearly 5 cm (2 in), are golden-yellow with yellow stamens and a whitish style. The globose fruits are coloured red and about 4 cm ($1^1/_2$ in) across. The seeds are large and dark grey to black.

It is not difficult to grow. It requires a nourishing compost. Water liberally and place in a sunny position in summer. In winter it requires light, dry conditions and a temperature of 5°-8°C (41°-46°F). Propagation from seed is a lengthy process, so taking cuttings is usually preferable. Detach a joint from the stem and leave it to dry. After about a week or 10 days insert in a pot filled with compost.

Echinofossulocactus
lloydii
Cactaceae

This (57) is one of 10 species of the genus Echinofossulocactus, all of which vary. They are native to Mexico. The name, derived from the Latin *echinus*, meaning hedgehog, and *fossula*, meaning furrow, reflects the characteristics of this genus. It is readily identified by the many narrow and wavy, lamella-like ribs. The ribs are not at first visible on young seedlings; they are formed only at the end of the first year. The upper spine is very striking — it is flat and papery. The flowers, emerging from the crown, have a short tube with numerous, naked, leathery-edged scales and white petals. *E. lloydii* is popular with growers because it flowers very early in the spring.

Cultivation is not difficult. These cacti require light, but not direct sun. Water very sparingly in winter. Propagate from seeds.

Chamaecereus
sylvestrii
(syn. *Lobivia sylvestrii*)
Cactaceae

Peanut Cactus (58) is native to the mountains of Argentina. It is found in almost every collection for it is undemanding and flowers profusely. It readily produces offshoots and forms thick clumps. The individual plants are about 10 cm (4 in) high and 1.5 cm (^{3}/$_5$ in) across. The soft cylindrical stem has six to ten ribs. The areoles have 10-15, bristly radial spines, 2 mm (^{1}/$_{10}$ in) long. The lovely flowers that emerge on the sides of the plant are more than 7 cm (2^3/$_4$ in) long. The bright vermilion red of the petals makes an attractive contrast with the yellow of the stamens.

For good growth, it requires free-draining, humus-rich soil and ample light. Provide cool and dry conditions in winter. When grown in full sun, the plants acquire a reddish tinge. In dry conditions they are susceptible to attack by pests.

Phyllocactus hybridus
'Ackermanii'
Cactaceae

Orchid cactus (59) is widely grown. This cultivar is also designated *Epiphyllum hybridum*. The original type species was epiphytic, twining over the bark of trees in the rain forests. That is why it requires more liberal watering in cultivation.

Adromischus cristatus
(syn. *Cotyledon cristatus*)
Crassulaceae

Crinkleleaf Plant (60) is an undemanding member of the family Crassulaceae. The genus Adromischus includes about 50 species widespread in South Africa. The opposite, cushion-like leaves are 40 mm (1^1/$_2$ in) long and 4-16 mm (^{1}/$_{10}$-^{2}/$_5$ in) wide, wedge-shaped towards the base, wavy on the margin, and completely covered with soft hairs. The racemose inflorescences are 15-20 cm (6-8 in) long. The individual flowers have a narrow, tubular calyx with short teeth and petals coloured whitish pink.

This species is easy to grow. Normal room temperature suits it well; in summer it tolerates high temperatures and in winter it tolerates temperatures as low as 5°C (41°F). In cool winter conditions restrict watering or withhold it completely. Feed every two to three weeks during the growing period. Repot after two years, but frequent repotting is not necessary. Propagate by de-

habit of growth

58

taching the fleshy leaves and leaving them to dry for a few days. As soon as the scar has healed, insert the leaf in compost or lay it on the surface. It will soon grow into a new plant.

Euphorbia obesa
Euphorbiaceae

The illustrated species (61) is native to South Africa where, however, it is now relatively rare because hundreds of specimens were dug up by collectors in the past. It was first brought to Europe in 1897. Spurges are extraordinarily diverse plants and their number includes both annual and perennial species, as well as herbaceous and woody plants. Some, such as *E. obesa*, resemble cacti. The stem is unbranched, spherical, 8-12 cm (3-5 in) across and divided into eight broad ribs. The entire stem is pale green to grey-green, with transverse purplish-red stripes. Small flowers arranged in a cyathium — the inflorescence characteristic of spurges — grow from a slight depression in the crown. When bruised all spurges exude a bitter milky sap.

Throughout the year it requires lots of light, and, in summer, sun and warmth. The growth period is in autumn. Water with care. Propagate from seed, which germinates rapidly and well, or by offshoots.

59

Euphorbia milii-
splendens 'Lutea'
(syn. *E. splendens*)
Euphorbiaceae

Crown of Thorns (62) is a very spiny shrub with succulent, branched stems. It is native to Madagascar, but has spread from there and became established in several tropical regions. The spines may be up to 1.5 cm ($^1/_2$-$2^3/_4$ in) long, are obovate, wedge-shaped at the base and completely glabrous. The inflor-

escences (cyathiums), composed of tiny inconspicuous flowers, are enclosed by two large, yellowish bracts. In the more commonly grown type species, the bracts are a vivid red.

This spurge is a lovely and thriving house plant. It grows extremely well in houses with central heating. It requires a sunny location throughout the year, preferably in a window. It grows best in a mixture of compost and sand. Water liberally during the growing period, but limit watering during the rest period from November to February, and again for about a month after the flowers have faded. Propagate by cutting off the tip of the stem, letting the milky sap that oozes out dry up and then inserting it in compost.

Echeveria
Crassulaceae

This is a very large genus, including about 150 species (63—a selection). In addition, there are numerous cultivars that make identification difficult. Members of the genus have a fairly wide range of distribution, extending from the southern part of North America through Central America to South America. Echeverias are grown chiefly for their decorative leaves which often form a ground rosette and are very succulent. They may be

61

Echeveria—vegetative
propagation by means of
leaves

**Echeveria setosa
'Doris Taylor'**
Crassulaceae

green, greyish-blue, or silvery-white; some are rusty brown because they have numerous hairs. Species with leaves that are wavy on the margin are popular with growers. The flowers are usually small and arranged in racemose inflorescences that may be up to 60 cm (24 in) high. They are variously coloured — white, pink, orange, greenish or carmine red.

Echeverias require dry conditions and a low winter temperature. Propagate by detaching a fleshy leaf and allowing it to dry for a short while. Insert in pure sand, where it will rapidly make roots. Alternatively, detach the young, lateral leaf rosettes. Propagation from seed takes longer, but the seeds germinate fairly rapidly at a temperature of 18°C (64°F).

This Echeveria (64) has no stem. The leaves are arranged in ground rosettes that are very thick, usually spherical or slightly flattened and about 15 cm (6 in) across. The slightly spoon-shaped leaves are 7-8 cm (2³/4-3 in) long and have blunt tips. They are strikingly hairy on both sides. The inflorescences are usually very rich, composed of numerous, small, reddish-yellow flowers. The cultivar 'Doris Taylor' has a compact inflorescence and exceptionally hairy leaves.

Indoor cultivation is very easy. All that Echeveria needs is adequate light and watering just so the soil does not become waterlogged. In summer it can be planted outdoors. It is often planted in ornamental patterns, with other species such as *E. elegans* and *E. derenbergii.*

Echeveria agavoides
Crassulaceae

This species (65), like most Echeverias, is native to Mexico. It has a very short stem, or none at all. The ground rosette, measuring about 15 cm (6 in), is composed of 15-25 leaves, broad at the base and narrowing towards pointed tips so that they are triangular in outline. They are 3-9 cm (1-3$\frac{1}{2}$ in) long, 2.5-5 cm ($\frac{3}{4}$-2 in) wide, very stiff, leathery and pale green, acquiring a reddish tinge when exposed to the sun. There is a brown spot on the tip. The reddish-yellow flowers are arranged in inflorescences up to 50 cm (20 in) high.

It is a popular house plant and very easy to grow. It requires

63

a nourishing compost. If possible, place the plant in or near a window, as it needs plenty of light, even in the winter. Water moderately in summer and sparingly in winter. The winter temperature should be 6°-8°C (43°-46°F). Propagate by detaching the readily produced side rosettes and rooting them in sandy compost. Even a leaf will root in this way.

Echeveria gibbiflora
Crassulaceae

This species (66) typically has long stems that may grow by as much as 10 cm (4 in) in summer, and by even more in optimum conditions. The leaf rosettes are spherical to slightly cylindrical and composed of about 20 leaves. These are spoon-like and ob-ovate, tipped with a point and keeled at the base. The striking grey-blue colour of the leaves changes to pink at the margins, even to red in the full sun. The bloom on their surface is very attractive. The inflorescences may reach a height of 50 cm (20 in) and are also entirely coated with a bloom. The flowers are about 25 mm (1 in) long and light red to pink in colour. New plants can rapidly be obtained from leaf cuttings or by detaching side rosettes. This is a very hardy Echeveria, suitable for planting in the rock garden in summer.

64

Cotyledon undulata
Crassulaceae

Silver Crown, Silver Ruffles (67). The most striking feature of this South African plant is its fleshy, almost orbicular leaves with a white chalky bloom which, however, rubs off if touched. The large, bell-shaped flowers grow from the tip of a long stem that may be up to 45 cm (18 in) high. They are always pendent and coloured orange-red, with 10 protruding stamens. Members of the genus Cotyledon were originally ranged in the genus Echeveria.

It requires a temperature of 10°-15°C (50°-59°F) in winter and adequate light and ventilation throughout the year. A heavy, clay-based compost with ample nutrients is best. The plants should be watered carefully from the base to avoid damaging the chalky bloom. It is readily propagated by detaching and rooting leaves or by stem cuttings.

Echeveria shaviana
Crassulaceae

This species (68) was introduced into cultivation from Mexico. It includes a great many cultivars which mainly differ in the coloration of the leaves, ranging from light brown to brownish-red. It forms a ground rosette of as many as 40 leaves. These are obovate and 4.5 cm (1⁴/5 in) long. They are 8 mm (³/10 in) wide at the base and 2.5 cm (1 in) wide at the opposite end, with a pointed, upcurved tip, rounded inward above, glabrous and rounded outwards beneath, and wavy on the margin. They are grey-green with a thick bloom, acquiring a pink tinge when exposed to the sun. The inflorescences, composed of 20-30 flowers, are erect, up to 30 cm (12 in) long and with a chalky bloom. The flowers, borne on stalks 2-3 mm (¹/10-¹/5 in) long, measure

12-15 mm ($^1/_2$-$^3/_5$ in). They are coloured pink outside, orange inside, and the petals are keeled outside. Only mature plants bear flowers.

Echeveria tolimanensis
Crassulaceae

This Echeveria (69) is native to the Toliman region of Mexico, where it usually grows in the shade of taller plants. It is a stemless species; its leaves are arranged in a ground rosette. They are very densely packed, fleshy, 4-8.5 cm (1$^1/_2$-3$^2/_5$ in) long, pointed at the tip and sometimes extend into a sharp, spiny point. They are completely coated with a chalky bloom. The racemose inflorescence is composed of 20-26 golden-yellow flowers. It is a very hardy species and stands up well to drought. Clay compost is a suitable substrate. It is readily propagated by seed. Propagation by leaf cuttings is poor. It is not cultivated as often as it deserves to be in view of its beauty and easy care.

Lithops pseudotruncatella var. volkii
Aizoaceae

Living Stone (70) truly resembles a pebble in appearance and coloration and is practically invisible in the stony wastes of its native South African habitat. *Lithops* is Greek for stone. It is also commonly called Pebble Plant. It is a splendid example of an organism's perfect adaptation to its environment. The body of such plants is composed of two opposite, fleshy leaves,

65

Lithops—plants prior to flowering

joined at the base and usually flattened at the top, as if truncated. In young plants, there is a narrow groove between the leaves which gradually opens and from which the flowers emerge. A new pair of fleshy leaves is formed each year. The previous year's leaves dry up and the remnants of these and of the flowers remain at the base of the plant. These should be removed. The colour of the flowers and the structure and coloration of the flat, terminal leaf surface are very important aids in identify-

67

ing the species of Lithops. At least 100 species have been described, of which about 40 are valid. *L. pseudotruncatella* typically has pale grey, branched markings on the flat surfaces of the leaves; in var. *volkii,* however, these markings are absent.

It requires a free-draining compost, ideally a mixture of well-rotted leaf mould, sand and pumice or stone rubble. A dry atmosphere and plenty of light are essential for healthy growth.

Do not water during the rest period from February to April, while the new plant takes its food from the dying parts of the old plant. Water by misting the soil from May onwards. Incorrect watering causes the greatest damage to the plants in cultivation. Do not allow water to remain on the leaves because they rot readily. The flowering period is generally in late summer and autumn. The golden yellow flowers of var. *volkii* bloom in July, opening in the afternoon. Lithops is easily propagated from seed. This may be obtained from your own plants, but it is necessary to grow several specimens of the same species and transfer the pollen with a brush. The seeds germinate readily in

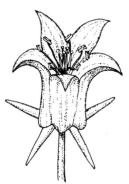

Echeveria
tolimanensis—flower

69

a mixture of peat and sand at a temperature of 20°C (68°F).
Flowers are not produced until after two to three years.

**Lithops
karasmontana
var. summitatum**
Aizoaceae

This Lithops (71) is native to the mountain regions of Namibia.
It spreads readily, forming extensive carpets. The body reaches
a height of 4 cm (1½ in) and is a pale grey colour. The flat tops
of the leaves are smooth or slightly wavy, 15-25 mm (½-1 in)
across, and coloured reddish-brown with reticulated markings.
The glossy white flowers measure up to 3.5 cm (1²/₅ in). Seedlings flower for the first time after three years at the end of the
growing period. The flowers are large — the same size as the
whole body. They open after midday.

91

Lithops turbiniformis
Aizoaceae

This species (72) was discovered in Cape Province in 1811. The plants grow singly or in pairs and do not form a carpet. It is only 2.5 cm (1 in) high. The flat leaf tops are almost circular, 2.5 cm (1 in) in diameter, coloured greyish-brown, reddish-brown or dark brown. They may be faintly furrowed, reticulated or even tubercled. The sides of the body are usually grey, occasionally yellowish-brown.

Faucaria tigrina
Aizoaceae

Tiger's Chaps (73) is one of about 33 species in the genus, all native to South Africa. Many hybrid varieties are cultivated because spontaneous cross-breeding often occurs when several are grown together. It is a succulent plant, usually without a stem. The leaf rosette is composed of several pairs of fleshy, decussate leaves joined together at the base. They are triangular and spiny-toothed on the margins (sometimes on the surface as well). There is a prominent keel on the underside of the leaves. The spines, which resemble the teeth of a tiger, gave the plant its specific and common names. The flowers are up to 5 cm (2 in) across and a brilliant yellow. They are numerous and produced from August to November.

This species does well indoors, if provided with adequate

71

72

sunlight. Water liberally in summer. It may be moved outdoors in summer, but must be sheltered from rain. In winter it requires a light and dry location at a temperature of 6°C (43°F). Faucarias may be propagated by division or from seed.

Conophytum pearsonii
Aizoaceae

This species (74) is a member of one of the largest genera of the family Aizoaceae. It is said to include as many as 300 species, some of which are among the smallest of flowering plants. *C. pearsonii* forms thick, cushion-like clumps of small club-shaped bodies about 1.5 cm (³/₅ in) high. The two opposite leaves are joined very near the top, the open groove being only 2-5 mm (¹/₁₀-²/₅ in) deep. The bright pinkish-violet flowers emerge from this. The whole plant is blue-green, with small, dark spots round the groove.

It is not difficult to grow but requires some experience. A suitable growing medium is a mixture of leaf mould and coarse sand. Water very moderately during the growing period from September to November. Give no water at all during the period of rest from January to June. During this period, a new pair of leaves develops inside the plant, which shrivels and does not look very pretty.

Pleiospilos nelii
Aizoaceae

This species (75) is one of 35 in the genus Pleiospilos, distributed throughout South Africa. Its body is superbly adapted to its environment. Like Lithops, Pleiospilos are deservedly called Living Stones. It is a stemless succulent plant with one or two pairs of opposite, decussate, very fleshy leaves that are semi-spherical and joined at the base. They are grey-green, marked with countless, dark, translucent dots. These gave the genus its name—the Greek *pleios* means many and *spilos* dots. The flowers may be up to 7 cm ($2^3/4$ in) across and are usually coloured yellow to salmon-pink.

A suitable growing medium is a mixture of leaf mould and sand. Water moderately during the growing period, from May to June, but the plant does not tolerate permanent wet and cool conditions. Keep absolutely dry in winter at a temperature of 10°-15°C (50°-59°F). With proper care, the plant will produce lovely, large blossoms that remain fresh a whole week. They remain closed in the morning, but open in the afternoon.

74

Crassula portulacea
Crassulaceae

This species (76) is one of 300 in the large genus Crassula. All are native to South Africa where they are widely distributed. Many are popular house plants because they are very decorative and quite easy to grow. *C. portulacea* is usually very branched and the short stems and branches of old specimens become woody. The succulent leaves are obovate, very glossy and crowded on the branches. The white, 5-merous flowers are arranged in terminal inflorescences. They are produced only by mature plants.

It grows well at normal room temperature, but it may be advisable to move it to a cooler, but still light, place in winter. The compost should be well-drained, with a sufficient amount of sand. Water quite liberally in hot weather but restrict watering as the temperature decreases. Propagate by stem cuttings or by placing a leaf on the surface of the compost.

Gasteria verrucosa
Liliaceae

This Gasteria (77), native to South Africa, is a very popular house plant with a long history. It was grown as a decorative plant in Europe as early as 1700. The genus Gasteria includes about 70 species. Identifying them is difficult because young plants are quite different from the adults. This species typically has a two-ranked arrangement of the leaves. These are very succulent, dark green in colour, 15-20 cm (6-8 in) long, pointed, grooved above, keeled on the under surface and dotted with white tubercles on both sides. The flowers are arranged in racemes that grow from the axils of the leaves. They are coloured red-green and are 3-merous, a feature indicating that Gasterias belong to the lily family. The swollen, belly-shaped, lower part of the flower tube gave rise to the name Gasteria (the Greek *gaster* means belly).

Cultivation is easy; it tolerates full sun both in summer and winter. It thrives at normal room temperature in summer. Keep at a temperature of about 10°C (50°F) in winter. Water quite liberally in hot weather and increasingly sparingly as the temperature decreases. Propagate by detaching the readily formed offshoots and inserting them into a free-draining sandy compost.

Pelargonium tetragonum
Geraniaceae

This sub-shrub (78) is a succulent member of the genus Pelargonium. In its native habitat in South Africa it reaches a height of 70 cm (28 in) but, when cultivated as a house plant, it is usually cut back to keep it shorter and to promote branching. The interesting, succulent stems have three or four angles, are pale green and glabrous. The five-lobed leaves are heart-shaped at the base and irregularly toothed on the margin. They drop at the end of the growing period. The sparse inflorescence usually consists of only two or three long-stalked flowers, which are coloured pink

75

76

and have prominent violet blotches. There is a marked difference in the size of the petals: the two upper petals are much bigger than the three lower ones.

During the growing period provide plenty of light (it tolerates direct sun), warmth and water. In winter, restrict watering, provide light and cooler conditions, about 15°C (59°F).

Pelargonium echinatum
Geraniaceae

The species (79) is another succulent Pelargonium from South Africa. It has an erect stem that is sparsely branched and woody. The stipules are typically 5 mm ($^1/_5$ in) long and prickly. The leaves have three to five lobes, are heart-shaped at the base, wavy on the margin and completely covered in soft, whitish hairs. They drop during the rest period. The flowers are pale violet; two petals have deep carmine-red blotches.

98

77

Agave ferox
Agavaceae

Agave (80) is a genus of very interesting succulent plants. Over 300 species are distributed from southern North Africa through Central to South America. Many are not suitable for growing as house plants because they are so big. However, quite large species can be cultivated successfully in glassed-in verandas or in conservatories. Young plants are very attractive but older specimens become a problem because of their huge size. *A. americana*, for example, is familiar as a decorative summer plant in parks, gardens and wherever there is ample space. Other very attractive species are *A. filifera*, with hair-like indumentum, and *A. victoriae-reginae* with white stripes on the spineless leaves. The leaf rosettes of *A. ferox* are 100 cm (39 in) across and are composed of numerous, stiff, dark green leaves with prickly margins. These 'teeth' are spaced 1-2 cm ($^2/_5$-$^4/_5$ in) apart and the terminal spine may be 2-3 cm ($^4/_5$-1 in) long. The inflorescence may be as much as 8-10 m (26-33 ft) high, with individual, pale yellow-green flowers up to 7 cm ($3^1/_2$ in) long.

They are easy to cultivate. Provide a free-draining compost and treat in the same way as plants of the genus Aeonium (see *A. nobile*, below).

Aeonium nobile
Crassulaceae

This plant (81) was introduced into cultivation from the Canary Islands. It has a very short stem topped by a huge leaf rosette that may be as much as 50 cm (20 in) across. The leaves are suc-

culent, up to 20-30 cm (8-12 in) long and 10-20 cm (4-8 in) wide.
The scarlet flowers grow from the axils of succulent stipules.

Adult plants require full sun; young plants should be shaded.
They stand up well to a dry atmosphere and should be watered,
in the morning or evening, only in extremely hot weather. In

winter, withhold water almost entirely and place the plants in a light position, with a temperature of about 8°C (46°F).

Pachyphytum oviferum
Crassulaceae

Moonstone Plant (82) resembles some Echeverias. This species is the most familiar of the eight belonging to the genus Pachyphytum, all native to Mexico. Although it is rarely grown as a house plant and is not much cultivated by growers of succulents, it deserves greater attention. It has a short, thick stem. The large, prominent, succulent leaves are obovate, 3-5 cm (1-2 in) long, up to 1.5 cm (½ in) thick and coated with a bluish bloom. The flowers, which appear in spring, are drooping and greenish with a pink throat.

It requires a light, well-ventilated position, at normal room temperature in summer and at 5°-10°C (41°-50°F) in winter. Water only when the compost is dry. Repot every other spring, taking care not to rub the bloom off the leaves. Propagate by detaching a leaf and allowing it to dry. Then lay it on the surface of the growing medium where it will soon root. After it has put out roots, pot it up in a small pot in clay compost.

81

Adenium obesum
Apocynaceae

The illustrated species (83) is native to South Africa, with a range extending to the southern part of the Arabian peninsula. Because it flowered only rarely, this small shrub did not become a popular house plant until growers grafted it on to oleander stock and so obtained profusely flowering specimens. The stems are usually crooked and terminated by clusters of obovate leaves, 3-10 cm (1-4 in) long and 3 cm (1 in) wide. The leaves are very glossy on the upper side and dull green beneath, faintly hairy at first, later glabrous. The flowers, arranged in umbels, are pink, with the petals edged a darker hue.

To encourage flowering, provide plenty of light throughout the year. The plant thrives at normal room temperature and can tolerate a lower temperature at night, so it can be moved outdoors to a sheltered spot in summer. Water liberally except in winter.

Senecio rowleyanus
Compositae

String-of-beads (84) is one of 3,000 species in the extraordinarily large genus Senecio. Many, such as cinerarias, are popular house plants. *S. rowleyanus* is a succulent species, native to South Africa. It resembles a string of pearls, for the weak, drooping stems are covered with numerous spherical leaves, pointed at the tip as well as at the base, and patterned with

translucent, longitudinal stripes. The flowers have a cinnamon-like scent. They are white with bright violet anthers.

It does best in a window where it has ample light. If the temperature remains above freezing point, the plant may be left in place even in winter. Excessive moisture will damage it, so water only when the compost is dry. It requires a nourishing, but free-draining, compost.

Senecio haworthii
(syn. *Kleinia tomentosa*)
Compositae

This species (85) of succulent Senecio is also native to South Africa. It is not a common house plant, but is often included in the collections of those who make succulents their hobby. Its erect stems, woody at the base, rise to a height of 70 cm (28 in). The alternate leaves are very succulent, narrowed at both ends, 2-4 cm ($^3/_4$-1$^1/_2$ in) long and about 1 cm ($^2/_5$ in) thick. The leaves and stems are thickly white-felted. The flowerheads are large and composed of numerous yellow flowers.

It does well in a light, sunny situation. Water liberally in summer, but restrict watering in winter. During the winter rest period, the plants are very sensitive to cold and damp conditions, which can destroy them. Propagate by detaching the individual stems and plant them in pots.

Senecio macroglossus
'Variegatus'
Compositae

This tufted plant (86) does not look as if it belongs to the genus Senecio, especially if judged by its leaves. It has weak, prostrate stems and leaves that resemble those of ivy. They are slightly succulent with pointed lobes. Those of the type species are dark green, but those of the cultivar 'Variegatus' have yellowish blotches. The blotches are very irregular and leaves on the same stem may range from ones that are completely yellow, through ones that are half yellow to some that are blotched only on the margins. The flowerheads are composed of about 15 flowers. The marginal ones are white, those in the centre are yellow.

This plant is most attractive if grown in a hanging container.

83

84

Propagate by stem cuttings taken with three or four leaves and insert them directly into compost.

Testudinaria elephantipes
Dioscoreaceae

This interesting plant (87) is native to South Africa and is found mainly in tropical and sub-tropical regions. Many species are food plants; their large, starchy, underground tubers are eaten like potatoes. The most striking feature of *T. elephantipes* is the huge root head covered with thick, corky tubercles, with six or seven angles. The stems are usually long and branched with alternate, kidney-shaped leaves with typical curving veins.

In winter, the top parts die back and the best temperature for the plant is 15°-18°C (59°-64°F). When growth is resumed in March or April, the temperature must be raised. Water moderately at first and liberally at the height of the growing season. Plenty of light is essential.

Sedum sieboldii
'Variegatum'
Crassulaceae

This Stonecrop (88) is native to Japan; it has been cultivated in Europe for several decades. It has slender, weak stems about 25 cm (10 in) long. The succulent leaves grow in whorls of three and are sessile, almost orbicular, and coloured blue-grey with red margins. The cultivar 'Variegatum' has white to yellow blotches on the leaves. The pink flowers are arranged in terminal inflorescences. After they have faded, usually in October, the shoots die back.

Transfer the plant to a cool place in October and water only very occasionally during the winter just to prevent the roots drying out. When new shoots begin to appear in April, the plant should be returned to its former light position.

Sedum morganianum
Crassulaceae

Burro's Tail (89) and the cultivar 'Burito' (90) are easy to care for and are popular house plants of Mexican origin. The drooping, branching stems, thickly covered with leaves, make the former an exceptionally good plant for windowboxes or hanging containers. The very succulent leaves are about 2 cm (^{2}/$_5$ in) long and pointed at the tip. They are pale green with a bluish bloom. The plant flowers rarely.

In summer, it thrives in a sunny and well ventilated position; it tolerates full sun. It also does very well if transferred to the garden. During the rest period, from November to January,

87

88

transfer it to a light place at a temperature of 5°-6°C (41°-43°F). At higher temperatures, the plants become unduly tall. Restrict watering in winter. Propagate by stem cuttings inserted into a sandy compost. Alternatively, detach individual leaflets and place them on the surface of the compost where they will readily put out roots.

The cultivar 'Burito' is a hardier plant with stronger stems. The succulent leaves are not flattened on the upper side so that they are almost circular in cross-section. It is cultivated in the same way as Burro's Tail.

90

**Kalanchoë
blossfeldiana**
Crassulaceae

This species (91) mostly bears blood-red flowers, but selective breeding has produced cultivars with creamy-yellow or violet flowers as well. It is native to Madagascar.

It requires a sunny position in summer and plenty of light even in winter. Because it flowers in winter, it requires some watering during the cold period.

Tradescantia pexata
(syn. *Tradescantia sillamontana*)
Commelinaceae

This species (92) differs markedly from the better-known members of the genus Tradescantia. Most are grown in water or compost in hanging containers, but *T. pexata* is a succulent species from Mexico. It makes low, thick cushions 10-15 cm (4-6 in) in diameter. The individual stems are only 5-6 cm (2-2½ in) long and thickly hairy. The plant's most ornamental feature is its foliage. The leaves are about 2 cm (¾ in) long, two-ranked, and surround the stem like a sheath. They are sharply keeled be-

111

neath and pointed at the tip. Their green surface is thickly covered with white hairs. The flowers have a hairy calyx composed of three sepals, three large pinkish-violet petals, and six prominent stamens with large yellow anthers and violet filaments.

It is grown in the same way as *T. navicularis* (see below). It is a pity that this Tradescantia is not found in indoor cultivation as often as it deserves. Far commoner house plants are *T. albiflora* with green leaves and white flowers, *T. fluminensis* with leaves conspicuously red beneath, and *T. blossfeldiana*, the red stems and the underside of the leaves of which are covered with whitish hairs.

Tradescantia navicularis
Commelinaceae

manner of spreading

This plant (93) is another of the three succulent species of the genus Tradescantia, which comprises about 30 species altogether. Its native habitat extends from Mexico to Peru. It is a much-branched plant with short, often rooting stems. The two-ranked leaves are sessile, arranged directly one above the other, and pointed. The surface is covered with white hairs. The plant's specific name refers to their shape, which resembles part of a ship. If it is grown in the sun, the leaves acquire a reddish tinge. Although it is a very interesting plant, it has one drawback in that it produces long shoots with sparsely spaced leaves that root readily as soon as they come in contact with the compost.

It requires a light location and tolerates direct sun. Water liberally in summer to keep the soil constantly moist. In winter, water only when the soil is dry. Repotting is inadvisable; it is better to renew the plant by means of cuttings, putting several of these in one pot.

92

Aloë brevifolia
Liliaceae

This species (94), like most members of this large genus (more than 200 species), is native to South Africa. They are popular house plants. Most people are familiar with *A. arborescens*, which is said to have medicinal properties. *A. brevifolia* is also widely grown. It forms carpeting clumps, for it readily produces offshoots. The leaves are arranged in ground rosettes 10-12 cm (4-5 in) in diameter. The succulent, narrowly-triangular leaves are 7-18 cm ($2^3/4$-7 in) long, 3 cm (1 in) wide and 1 cm ($^2/5$ in) thick. They are slightly rounded inward above, faintly keeled beneath and have ornamental spines, 2-3 cm ($^3/4$-1 in) long, on the margins. The attractive inflorescences are up to 50 cm (20 in) high and composed of numerous small flowers.

Because it is so easy to grow, this is a most rewarding plant. It merely requires a light position and, in summer, may be transferred to the garden or balcony. It requires a lime-free, very sandy compost. Water very moderately and take care to avoid wetting the leaves as they rot readily. In winter, it requires light and rather cool conditions. Propagate by means of the offshoots. Detach the young plantlets and pot up.

Stapelia gigantea
Asclepiadaceae

Stapelias (95) are South African plants with short, succulent stems that often branch to form a carpet. Their most attractive feature are their large flowers which grow from the base of the plant, only rarely at the top. Their disadvantage, however, is their unpleasant odour. The stems of *S. gigantea* are winged on the edges and covered with minute, distant teeth. The long-stalked flowers may be up to 35 cm (14 in) across. The corolla lobes have long, very narrow points; they are pale yellow with short, black, wavy, transverse stripes.

94

97

It is an undemanding plant that will grow in sun as well as
partial shade, in heavy, clay soil as well as in light, sandy compost. In winter, either transfer the plant to a cool position and
water very sparingly, or leave it in its permanent location and
water normally. Propagation by vegetative means or from seeds
is not difficult. Separate stem segments and leave them to dry
for several days before inserting them in compost. Seeds will
germinate at a temperature of 20-25°C (68°-77°F).

98

Stapelia grandiflora
Asclepiadaceae

This Stapelia (96) has quadrangular stems covered with fine hairs. The edges have spiny teeth spaced far apart. These teeth bear minute, scale-like leaves that soon drop. The flowers, about 15 cm (6 in) in diameter, are flat with short tubes and covered with long hairs. The corolla lobes are dark purple above with yellowish transverse stripes, and blue-green beneath.

Stapelia variegata
Asclepiadaceae

The Carrion Plant (97, 98) is the most common species of Stapelia. It readily cross-breeds with the other species. It forms large clumps of fleshy stems coloured green or grey-green, often reddish. The flowers, sometimes as many as five, are 5-9 cm (2-3½ in) across and appear in late summer or early autumn. The corolla lobes, spotted yellow and brown, are broadly ovate, bluntly pointed at the tip, and transversely tubercled so that they appear to be wrinkled. The marked variability of the flowers is why the species includes many varieties. Var. *atropurpurea* (98) has brownish-red tubercles on the corolla lobes.

118

Ceropegia woodii
—end of stem with flower
and fruit

99

***Ceropegia
stapeliaeformis***
Asclepiadaceae

The genus Ceropegia (99) includes about 155 species that are not easy to identify. *C. woodii* is the one most commonly grown as a house plant. *C. stapeliaeformis* is a liana with a very fleshy stem up to 1.5 m (59 in) long. The leaves are small and scale-like; they soon drop, leaving the stems bare. The fascinating flowers may be up to 6 cm (2¹/₂ in) long and are usually borne in clusters of four.

Grow the plant in a mixture of humus, leaf mould and sand. It requires a light, warm and well ventilated position. In summer water liberally, in winter sparingly, in accordance with the temperature. Propagate by means of the creeping or trailing stems, which root readily when they come in contact with the compost.

119

ORCHIDS

People generally think of orchids in the context of lush, tropical vegetation, but many species are found not only in sub-tropical regions, but also in cooler parts of the world, even beyond the Arctic Circle. The orchid family (Orchidaceae) is one of the largest in the whole plant kingdom. Species differ not only in the shape of the body, but also in their ways of life.

Some species lack chlorophyll and cannot, therefore, photosynthesize organic compounds. Instead, they live in symbiotic association with the mycelium of a fungus. This phenomenon is called mycorrhiza. It is an important factor in the life of all orchids, particularly in the early stages of development — during germination. It has probably something to do with the transfer of enzymes. Orchid seeds contain hardly any reserve stores of food. The filaments of the mycelium penetrate the root cells of the orchid and multiply there. The plant cells feed on the contents of the filaments. Adult orchids with a sufficiently large leaf area to produce their own food by photosynthesis soon cease to depend on the fungus. Orchids that lack chlorophyll, however, are dependent on the symbiotic association with the fungus throughout their lives.

Some species of orchids are epiphytic, that is, they grow on other plants without obtaining any benefits from them or doing them any harm. Others are terrestrial, that is, they grow on the ground. Many have rhizomes or tubers; others have no roots of any sort. Stems may be erect or drooping, jointed or without joints, covered with leaves or leafless.

The most ornamental feature of orchids is the flower. The flowers always have only one plane of symmetry and an inferior ovary that develops into a capsule. The showy and often fragrant flowers attract insects but they are deceptive blossoms, for they do not produce nectar.

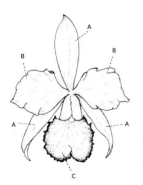

Schematic diagram of an orchid blossom
(Cattleya):
A) perianth segments of the outer ring,
B) perianth segments of the inner ring,
C) lip

100

101

102

Paphiopedilum insigne
Orchidaceae

The cultivars 'Sandereae' (100) and 'Harefield Hall' (101) are shown here. This species is native to the Himalayas.

    Paphiopedilum orchids are distributed throughout the tropical and sub-tropical regions of southeast Asia, and include some 50-60 species, plus numerous cultivars. Members of this genus have large, usually solitary flowers. The slipper-shaped lip is their most striking feature. The scape grows from a rosette. It flowers from autumn until spring. The flowers are up to 10 cm (4 in) across. For cultivation details, see *P. concolor* (below).

Paphiopedilum concolor
Orchidaceae

This species (102) is native to Vietnam, Thailand and Burma. The leaf rosette is composed of dark green leaves, marbled grey-green above and reddish-brown beneath. The scape, usually

122

103

with a single flower, is up to 100 cm (39 in) tall and thickly covered with reddish hairs. The flowers are 6-8 cm (2½-3 in) across and coloured ochre-yellow spotted with violet. They are very long-lasting, remaining on the plant for 6-10 weeks, or for a slightly shorter time when cut and put in a vase.

P. concolor grows well in a mixture of osmunda fibre, fresh sphagnum moss, crushed bark and dried oak leaves. Growers often prepare their own mixtures, based on experience. Whatever medium you choose it is important that it is free-draining. Water regularly, as paphiopedilums have no storage organs — pseudobulbs — and so no period of rest; the growing medium must never become dry. The temperature of the environment depends on the species. In general, paphiopedilums with marbled leaves require higher temperatures — a minimum of 17°C (63°F).

Paphiopedilum
fairrieanum
Orchidaceae

This species (103) has, perhaps, the most beautiful flowers of the whole genus. It was brought to Europe from Bhutan in 1857, but it died as a result of improper cultivation by the first growers. It was not cultivated again for 50 years.

It is a lime-loving species and so lime should be added to the substrate. Roots and shoots begin growing from about April, when it requires regular misting to increase humidity. Provide good ventilation and light shade from spring onwards. Increase day and night ventilation in summer. The autumn and winter temperature should be 15°-18°C (59°-64°F) during the day and 15°C (59°F) at night. Once the flowers have died, reduce watering.

Paphiopedilum
callosum
Orchidaceae

This species (104), native to Thailand, is distinguished by marbled leaves and a scape, 25-30 cm (10-12 in) high, which bears one or two flowers 8-12 cm (3-5 in) across. It is a thermo-

104

105

philous orchid. It requires a temperature of at least 18°-22°C (64°-72°F); ideally 22°-26°C (72°-79°F).

Oncidium papilio
Orchidaceae

Butterfly Orchid (105) is distributed in Venezuela, Peru, Ecuador, Colombia and Trinidad. The genus Oncidium is one of the largest genera of epiphytic orchids. The shape and colour of the flowers make them seem like some exotic butterfly (the Latin

106

papilio means butterfly). Although in some Oncidiums the pseudobulbs are reduced or absent, those of this species are well developed. A leaf, 15-18 cm (6-7 in) long with faint reddish blotches, grows from each one. The thin, firm scapes are terminated by a single flower about 8 cm (3 in) across, conspicuous by the three erect, linear perianth segments up to 12 cm (4³/₄ in) in length. This is a thermophilous species and the conditions for growing are the same as for Cattleyas (see below).

Angraecum
sesquipedale
Orchidaceae

This epiphyte (106) belongs to a genus of about 50 species that grow in Africa and Madagascar. The blue-green leaves are fleshy and covered with a waxy coat. The scanty inflorescences

107

are composed of two to four white flowers, 12-15 cm (4³/₄-6 in) across.

This orchid requires very warm conditions. The optimum temperature in spring and summer is 20°-26°C (68°-79°F), in winter 17°-22°C (63°-72°F). Mist regularly in summer. The growing medium should be a mixture of fern roots, fresh sphagnum moss, beech leaves and charcoal.

**Angraecum
eichlerianum**
Orchidaceae

The scapes are up to 1 m (39 in) long, the leaves (107) are long and elliptic and the short-stalked flowers are either solitary or in pairs. The perianth segments are pale green. The lip is shell-shaped, broad, and coloured white with a greenish-yellow throat. The spur is about 4.5 cm (1³/₄ in) long and geniculate.

Cultivate in the same way as *A. sesquipedale* (see above). It grows well in a hanging basket, perforated pot or even on a cork tile to which some kind of organic material is affixed.

Miltonia—hybr.
Orchidaceae

Pansy Orchid (108) is a tropical epiphyte native to Brazil and Colombia. It has short pseudobulbs, usually bearing two leaves, and upright racemes of few flowers. These are a veritable kaleidoscope of colour. The perianth segments are typically all flat and practically identical, reminiscent of pansies. Miltonias are very ornamental indoor plants, but they are not suitable for cutting because the flowers last only a few hours.

To provide the right conditions for growth, it is necessary to know the place of origin of the species, for Brazilian and Colombian species have different requirements. The first group in-

127

cludes *M. anceps* and *M. candida,* which require warm, shaded conditions and liberal watering in summer; during the rest period, water only to keep the soil moist. The second group, which includes *Miltoniopsis vexillaria* and *M. phalaenopsis,* requires cooler conditions; these orchids are grown at a temperature of about 18°C (64°F). Hybrids of both groups are grown in the same way.

Cattleya—hybr.
Orchidaceae

Cattleya (109, 113) is a South American genus with 40-50 species, hundreds of varieties, and countless hybrids, the result of both spontaneous and selective cross-breeding. They are divided into two groups. The first includes thermophilous, bifoliate species, that is, those with two leaves growing from the pseudobulbs. They have smaller, more numerous flowers. They flower without a rest period after the pseudobulbs have formed. *C. intermedia* is an example of this group. The second, unifoliate group includes Cattleyas that require a rest period between the time that the pseudobulbs are fully developed and the formation of the flowers. *C. labiata* is an example of this group. The rare cultivar 'Golden Jay' (113) is noteworthy for the unusual colour combination of the perianth segments and the lip.

Repot in the third or fourth year between March and June,

109

when new roots and shoots start to grow. Remove old pseudo-bulbs that are without leaves and roots. Leave at least three healthy pseudobulbs on the plant.

**× *Brassocattleya*
'Madame Marons'**
Orchidaceae

Because Brassavola and Cattleya are generically close, cross-breeding is very simple and the result is the intergeneric hybrid × Brassocattleya. It is readily identified by the fringe along the entire perimeter of the lip. Cattleya, of course, can also be cross-bred with other genera, for example with Laelia; the hybrid obtained from this crossing is called × Laeliocattleya. These cultivars come in a wide range of colours and their cultivation is the same as that of thermophilous Cattleyas. The cultivar illustrated (110) has deep pinkish-violet flowers, the inside of the lip is yellow.

Cattleya intermedia
Orchidaceae

This orchid (111, 112) is very popular with growers because of its large, magnificent flowers and their longevity. It is native to Brazil. The large, narrow pseudobulbs produce two leaves. The inflorescence is composed of two to eight flowers; these are borne practically without a break from spring until autumn. The

129

110

Cattleya intermedia on a trunk

cultivar 'Alba' (111) differs from the type species (112) by having white blossoms.

Conditions for growing both the white-flowered cultivar and the type species are the same. The spring temperature should be 20°-27°C (68°-81°F). Shade the plants from too much sun. Good ventilation is essential. In summer the room should be aired frequently, even at night, and the temperature should not fall below 30°C (86°F). The winter temperature should be 18°-23°C (64°-73°F) during the day and 13°-16°C (55°-61°F) at night. Water liberally and mist frequently; do not allow the plant to become too dry during the growing season. Maintain high humidity — at least 50 per cent — even in winter, and never water the plant with hard water.

Cattleya—hybr.
Orchidaceae

'Golden Jay' (113). See Cattleya—hybr. (109) above.

Cymbidium—hybr.
Orchidaceae

Cymbidiums (114) are readily grown indoors. The genus Cymbidium includes some 50 species distributed from Madagascar through India to Japan and south to Australia. They usually have very short stems, thickly covered with leathery leaves and flowers arranged in spikes. They are good for cutting; the flow-

130

111

ers are very long-lasting. Too vigorous growth may be a problem. Plants can reach a height of 1 m (39 in) and produce leaves up to 70 cm (28 in) long. Horticulturists, therefore, try to develop low-growing forms.

They are mostly terrestrial orchids and so grow well in pots. They even have no special compost requirements. Many cymbidiums like cool conditions. Maintain a temperature of 10°-16°C (50°-61°F) during the rest period after flowering.

Phalaenopsis amboinensis
Orchidaceae

This epiphyte (115) is one of 40-50 species of Phalaenopsis, distributed throughout India, Malaysia, the Philippines, New Guinea and northern Australia. They do not have pseudobulbs and the stem is greatly suppressed. The leaves are leathery. The perianth segments are either all the same size, or else the ones forming the inner ring are larger. The illustrated species is a rather small plant with a rosette of small leaves. The flowers are white and each perianth segment has pale pink transverse stripes. It is native to the Moluccas.

131

112

In its native habitat, *P. amboinensis* grows on the trunks of trees in shade and in a humid atmosphere. As a result, it is sensitive to dry conditions and low temperatures. In winter it requires a temperature of 17°-21°C (63°-70°F). Keep the root ball constantly wet. The temperature must be increased from spring onwards. By summer it should reach 28°C (82°F) in the shade; at night it should not fall below 20°C (68°F). The plants do well in baskets or perforated pots in a mixture of osmunda root, fresh sphagnum moss and crushed beech leaves. They should be watered only with soft water. The atmospheric humidity should be at least 60 per cent but 70 per cent is preferable.

Vanda teres
Orchidaceae

Vandas (116) are readily identified even outside the flowering period by their erect stems, up to 1 m (39 in) high, covered with alternate leaves on two sides, and numerous aerial roots. There are some 60-70 species of Vanda distributed from India to New Guinea. The perianth segments are almost identical and narrow towards the base in a shape like a fingernail. The lip has a short spur, the middle lobe is kidney-shaped.

It stands up well to direct sun, requiring light shading only on the hottest summer days. Maintain a temperature of about 25°-27°C (77°-81°F). Mist frequently to provide high humidity. In late summer, limit watering and reduce the temperature to 17°-22°C (63°-72°F). Too little light and warmth prevent the plants flowering because the buds drop prematurely.

Vanda × rothschildiana
Orchidaceae

This hybrid species (117) is derived from crossing *V. coerulea* with *V. sanderana*. It is particularly in the large-scale cultivation of Vandas that use is made not only of interspecific, but also of intergeneric hybrids. Vanda species are most often crossed with species of the genus Ascocentrum; the resulting intergeneric hybrid is designated ×Ascocenda. It is distinguished by large flowers, striking colours, and smaller habit. This hybrid is noted for its large flowers, 8-15 cm (3-6 in) across, which are a lovely amethyst blue with darker markings. They are relatively long-lasting.

Vandas can readily be propagated by vegetative means. There are two methods. The first is by detaching the sideshoots produced by older plants as soon as they form their own roots. The second method is by dividing the stem if it has already formed aerial roots along its length. Cut off the top part of the stem and insert it in a growing medium. Leave the lower part in the original substrate, where it will soon produce a new sideshoot.

Vanda tricolor var. suavis
Orchidaceae

This species (118) is found only on the island of Java. It is extremely variable and several sub-specific units have been described, one of them being the illustrated variety. The stem may be as much as 1.5 m (59 in) high and is thickly covered with leaves. The leaves are strap-shaped and 30-50 cm (12-20 in) long. The inflorescence overtops the leaves and is composed of

113

114

eight to ten flowers. These are about 7 cm (2³/₄ in) across and pleasantly scented. The flowering period is from May to September.

For good growth, provide a free-draining substrate, such as a coarse mixture of fern roots, crushed oak bark, fresh sphagnum moss and organic fertilizer. This orchid requires a very humid atmosphere. Do not reduce watering until late summer. In winter it requires a temperature of 17°-22°C (63°-68°F). If the plant does not produce flowers it is usually because it lacks sufficient light; if the buds drop, that is the result of too cool conditions.

Coelogyne pandurata
Orchidaceae

This species (119) is native to Borneo and Sumatra, where it grows on trees alongside rivers. The pseudobulb is cylindrical and produces two leaves about 35 cm (14 in) long. The very fragrant flowers are arranged in loose, drooping inflorescences.

115

Because it is an epiphytic orchid, it requires a light and aerated substrate for good growth — a mixture of fern roots, crushed oak bark, fresh sphagnum moss and organic fertilizer is ideal. Some species grow well in a flat dish. All require adequate ventilation. They may be grown in a plant-case and also on a flower stand by a window.

Lycaste aromatica
Orchidaceae

The genus Lycaste (120) is native to tropical America. It was named after Lycaste, daughter of Priam, the legendary king of Troy at the time of the Trojan war. It includes about 35 species that mostly grow as epiphytes on trees. The ovoid pseudobulbs with two thin, deciduous leaves, are characteristic. The numerous flowers are long-stalked, about 3-5 cm (1-2 in) across and very fragrant. It requires a lightly shaded position and nourishing, but free-draining, compost. A good mixture is fern roots, fresh sphagnum moss, leaf mould or rotted turves, charcoal and crushed brick. Provide plenty of ventilation and mist the plant liberally during the growing period. After the leaves have

117

118

119

dropped, mist just enough to prevent the pseudobulbs shrivelling and drying up.

Pleione formosana
Orchidaceae

Pleiones include both epiphytic and terrestrial orchids, found in the mountains of Asia from the Himalayas to Taiwan. They have globose or ovoid pseudobulbs from which grow narrow leaves and scapes. The leaves are slightly leathery and drop before the resting period. The flowers grow singly or in pairs. The species illustrated (121) is large compared to others in the genus; the pseudobulbs are up to 10 cm (4 in) across, the leaves up to 35 cm (14 in) long and the flowers may be up to 10 cm (4 in) across.

During the growing period, keep the plant at normal room temperature. After the leaves have dropped, the temperature should be slightly lower. Pleiones are not very pretty when they have finished flowering and, therefore, it is advisable to move them to a partially shaded spot in the garden. They must be sheltered from direct sun. The pseudobulbs should be overwintered in a cellar and watered sparingly. As soon as they begin new growth, move them to a window and water liberally. Propagation is by the readily produced small pseudobulbs, called bulbils.

Dendrobium nobile
Orchidaceae

The vast number of species — some 2,000 — indicates the variability of this genus. Dendrobiums are epiphytic orchids found from the Himalayas to Japan and southward to New Zealand. The stem of *D. nobile* (122) is up to 60 cm (24 in) high, fleshy, and covered with narrow leaves that remain on the plant for two years. The flowers usually grow in twos or threes from the nodes and are 7-10 cm (2³/₄-4 in) across.

This orchid does well indoors. After flowering, it should be watered sparingly until new shoots begin to form. Moving the

120

121

plants to a shaded spot in the garden for the summer has proved to be very beneficial.

Dendrobium victoriae-reginae
Orchidaceae

This (123) is a very ornamental member of the large genus Dendrobium. The generic name means 'living on a tree' (The Greek *dendron*=tree and *bioein*=to live), reflecting the epiphytic way of life of all these orchids. The flowers with their large, spreading petals are typical of *D. victoriae-reginae*.

Repot only after two years. It is better to put the plants in a smaller container in a free-draining substrate. Even though they require a great deal of water, the soil must not be sodden. Hard water is very harmful. Dendrobiums require a humid atmosphere for a good growth — a relative humidity of about 50 per cent in winter and 70 per cent in summer should be provided; use rainwater if possible.

140

122

123

124

Phragmopedium longifolium
Orchidaceae

This species (124) is found in rather damp, rocky habitats in Costa Rica, Panama and Colombia. It may occur at elevations of up to 2,000 m (6,600 ft) and grows either as an epiphyte on old trees or as a terrestrial orchid in humus-rich soil. The structure of the flowers resembles that of the flowers of the related genus Paphiopedilum. The two side segments are very narrow and long, coloured violet, and loosely coiled in a spiral. The central segment is upright and brown in colour, with darker, longitudinal stripes. The lip is large, pouch-like, coloured yellow edged with white and with green markings inside. The stem is thickly covered with numerous leathery leaves.

It likes cool conditions — a temperature of about 23°C (73°F)

125

in summer and 15°-18°C (59°-64°F) in winter. Ventilate well and mist frequently.

Brassia verrucosa
Orchidaceae

The flowers (125) measure up to 10 cm (4 in) and have long, extremely narrow segments coloured yellow-green with minute black spots. The lip, shaped like a cornucopia, is white with brownish markings. Unfortunately, these ornamental blossoms have an unpleasant odour. The inflorescences, composed of 10-15 flowers, are up to 60 cm (24 in) long.

This orchid should be grown at normal room temperature, but requires a markedly cooler temperature at night. Ventilate well. Water freely from spring to autumn, and more sparingly in winter; never allow the compost to dry out. Use only soft water.

143

126

Propagate the plants when repotting; detach and plant healthy pseudobulbs, which will soon form new plants.

Ansellia africana
Orchidaceae

Ansellias (126) are native to tropical Africa. There are only six species, *A. africana* being the most familiar. It is an epiphyte with firm, grooved stems and narrow leaves, up to 40 cm (16 in) long, with five pronounced ribs. The inflorescences are branched, more than 50 cm (20 in) long, the flowers 4-6 cm (1½-2½ in) across.

It thrives indoors and forms upward-growing aerial roots. Maintain a maximum summer temperature of 20°C (68°F) and water liberally. Late summer marks the beginning of the rest period; reduce watering and provide the plant with cooler conditions, about 16°-20°C (61°-68°F).

144

128

× Vuylstekeara
Orchidaceae

This orchid (127) is a triple intergeneric hybrid derived from Cochlioda × Miltonia × Odontoglossum and developed in 1912. It grows to a height of more than 1 m (39 in) and the size of the inflorescence is about 75 cm (30 in) in length.

It grows well indoors if placed in a window. In winter, maintain a daytime temperature of about 18°C (64°F) and a nighttime temperature of 13°C (55°F). Liberal watering is essential, as the plant must not be allowed to dry up even in winter.

Epidendrum cochleatum
Orchidaceae

The genus Epidendrum includes 1,000 species distributed in the tropical and sub-tropical regions of the Americas. The generic name is of Greek origin and means 'on a tree' (*epi* = on, *dendron* = tree), suggesting that members of this genus are epiphytes. They have narrow pseudobulbs, leaves that, as a rule, are leathery, and terminal inflorescences. *E. cochleatum* (128) has pseudobulbs about 10 cm (4 in) long, bearing two leaves. These are elongate, about 20 cm (8 in) long. The upright inflorescences are usually composed of five to eight flowers. The perianth segments are linear, up to 4 cm (1½ in) long, and coloured white and green; the lip is violet and black, marked yellow.

Provide the plant with light to partly shaded conditions and

146

a normal room temperature; in winter the temperature should not fall below 15°C (59°F). During the growing period, water when the surface of the compost is dry. Limit watering as soon as the shoots ripen in the autumn. Propagate the plant when re-potting by detaching healthy pseudobulbs which may develop into flower-bearing plants within two to three years.

Odontoglossum
cervantesii
Orchidaceae

This orchid (129) grows as an epiphyte in the mountain forests of Mexico and Guatemala. The pseudobulbs are small, 2-3 cm (³/₄-1 in) long, slightly compressed and faintly angled in the lower part. A single leaf, 10-15 cm (4-6 in) long, grows from the top of the pseudobulb. The flowers, are arranged in racemes that are always pendent. They are 4-6 cm (1½-2¼ in) across, white, occasionally tinged with pink, and with brownish-violet stripes at the base of the segments.

This species requires a relatively low temperature in winter 14°-16°C (57°-61°F) in the daytime, 12°C (54°F) at night. It is readily propagated by detaching the pseudobulbs when repot-ting. Wrap sphagnum moss round the pseudobulbs and put them in a plastic bag until the first roots appear.

129

FOLIAGE PLANTS

Their fresh greenery embracing a wide range of tones, their striking and frequently unusual habit, and the decorative effects of their graceful fronds and lush foliage are
what makes ferns and selaginellas such favourite house plants.

Most ferns grow in shady and damp locations. Many are indigenous to tropical rain
forests. Their number includes epiphytes which grow on the trunks and branches of
trees. On the other hand, there are also ferns that grow in locations that are definitely
dry, even though shaded or at least partially shaded, such as rock crevices. Another
extreme environment is by water and marshes.

Ferns do not produce flowers and, therefore, neither fruits nor seeds. They repro-
duce by means of spores, produced in abundance as a very fine powder in sporangia
growing on the undersides of the leaves. Whereas a seed develops directly into
a young plant resembling the parent, a fern spore that falls to the ground first develops
into a prothallium, a flat body measuring only a few millimetres. This bears the organs
that produce the male and female sex cells and is where fertilization takes place. Only
a fertilized egg cell can develop into the graceful fronds of a fern.

Selaginellas are usually inhabitants of tropical rain forests; only a few grow in the
temperate zone. Their stems are forked and thickly covered with small, scale-like
leaves that vary according to the position in which they grow. Those that grow in the
axils of the forks are symmetrical. The other leaves on the stems are faintly asymmetrical. A leafless organ, called a rhizophore, grows downward at the point where the stem
branches. At the tips of the stems there are small cones composed of sporophylls,
bearing on their upper sides a kidney-shaped sporangium filled with spores.

130   131

Pteris cretica—leaflet
with recurved margin
sheltering the sori

132

Nephrolepis exaltata
Nephrolepidaceae

The genus Nephrolepis includes about 30 species, some of which are epiphytic, others terrestrial. *N. exaltata* (130) has graceful arching fronds up to 80 cm (31½ in) long and divided into numerous fine segments. The young fronds, like those of all ferns, are tightly furled inwards, unfurling as they grow. Besides the type species, many cultivars are grown. These differ in the division of the leaf blade, in the individual leaflets (which may be wavy, flat or straight), in their habit of growth, or in the size of the clumps. The cultivar 'Hillii', with bipinnately compound, narrow, crowded leaflets is very lovely. 'Rooseveltii' has wavy leaflets; 'Whitmanii' has very fine, multipinnately compound leaflets; 'Teddy Junior' has wavy, furled leaflets coloured dark green.

This fern tolerates ample light and normal room temperature. It does not require a very humid atmosphere. In fact it is more seriously affected by too much water rather than by occasional drying out. Feed during the growing period. The recommended growing medium is a mixture of two parts peat, two parts leaf mould and one part sand. *N. exaltata* can also be grown by hydroponics. Propagate by dividing clumps when repotting or by means of the plant's runners. When these come in contact with the compost they put out roots. After they have been detached from the parent plant, they will develop into new individuals.

Platycerium bifurcatum
Polypodiaceae

The genus Platycerium includes 18 species from tropical forests throughout the world, mostly in Asia, less often in the Americas. *P. bifurcatum* (131) is native to the forests of Australia and Polynesia, where it grows as an epiphyte on trees. It is a very interesting fern with two types of leaves. One kind is kidney-shaped to orbicular, green at first, later brown, adpressed to the trunks of trees. These serve to hold the plant to the support and also to capture humus and water. The second kind is forked, green, with rusty-brown sporangia on the underside. The silvery tint of the leaves is produced by numerous stellate trichomes which are visible only with the aid of a microscope.

The recommended growing medium is a mixture of compost, coarse peat and crushed beech leaves. Platyceriums do well in pots, wooden baskets and on sheets of bark, as well as on epi-

Platycerium growing on the bark of a tree

133

134

phyte stumps, in plant-cases and greenhouses. In summer, shade it from direct sun. It thrives in houses with central heating because it requires rather warm conditions, even in winter. Misting the leaves is very beneficial.

Pteris cretica
'Albolineata'
Pteridaceae

Variegated Table Fern (132) was brought to Europe in 1860 from the botanical garden in Java. The genus Pteris includes about 280 species found in tropical and subtropical regions; the range of some extends even into the temperate zone. Many cultivars with differently coloured leaves and different growth habits are grown as house plants. The cultivar 'Albolineata' has broader leaflets striped with white. It grows to a height of 30-50 cm (12-20 in). The leaves are composed of several, linear-lanceolate leaflets, slightly wavy on the margins and recurved on the undersides.

It grows well in a mixture of peat, humus and sand. It is often grown with other plants in ceramic dishes, glass demijohns or fish-bowls. It has no special temperature or light requirements but does best in partial shade. In winter it tolerates temperatures as low as 10°-12°C (50°-54°F). Propagate by means of the spores, which germinate well on pure peat at a temperature of 22°C (72°F). Young plants require plenty of light and moisture.

Adiantum macrophyllum
Adiantaceae

Maidenhair Ferns (133) are among the loveliest of all. There are approximately 200 species distributed mainly in South America. The pinnate leaves are composed of numerous leaflets with faintly curved margins and sori on the underside. The sori are green at first, turning dark brown when ripe. The large leaves with four to six pairs of leaflets, almost rhomboid in outline, are typical. It is a shade-loving plant and is fairly demanding in terms of water and humidity.

It does well at a temperature of 18°-20°C (64°-68°F) in winter, but tolerates temperatures up to 25°C (77°F). It must never dry out, so water regularly even in winter. Repot after two years, at which time it can be propagated by division.

Adiantum tenerum
Adiantaceae

This species (134) is a very decorative, though tender, house plant, native to the rain forests of tropical South America. Numerous cultivars, which are hardier than the type species, are commonly grown as house plants. The most familiar is probably 'Scutum Roseum', with leaflets coloured deep red when young. There is also one species, *A. capillus-veneris*, with a range that extends from the tropics into Europe; it can be found on the At-

136

lantic seaboard and in the Mediterranean region. It has black
stalks and triangular leaves, 80 cm (31 in) long and 50 cm (20 in)
wide, that are multipinnate with very thin, wedge-shaped leaflets bluntly toothed at the tips.

It requires an environment as similar as possible to its natural
habitat. Very high humidity is especially important so a Wardian case or other glass-enclosed space is ideal. Propagate by dividing older plants or by means of spores.

Pellaea rotundifolia
Sinopteridaceae

Although the genus Pellaea has about 80 species, this (135) is
the only one grown in Europe. It is native to the woodlands of
New Zealand. The simply pinnate leaves are about 20-30 cm
(8-12 in) long, with alternate, nearly orbicular, leathery, dark
green, very short-stalked leaflets. The axis of the leaves is conspicuously hairy. The sori grow on the margins of the leaflets
and are coloured brown.

When grown indoors, it tolerates direct sun in summer. In
winter, it does well at normal room temperature, but will tolerate a temperature of 8°-15°C (46°-59°F). It is sensitive to an

154

excessively humid atmosphere. Feed from spring to summer. Propagate by means of spores.

Blechnum gibbum
Blechnaceae

This species (136) has a rhizome up to 1 m (39 in) high, resembling a stem and topped by a thick rosette of large leaves. The general effect is reminiscent of a palm tree. The pinnatifid leaves with delicate segments are coloured a lovely fresh green.

Even though this species of hard fern is very decorative, it is not often grown indoors because it has quite demanding requirements. It needs light, but not direct sunlight. Providing adequate humidity can be a problem. Letting the compost dry can also kill the plant. In winter, the temperature must not fall below 18°C (64°F). Draughts are also dangerous. Therefore, the best place for growing this fern is a glass-enclosed space, such as a plant-case if the specimen is a small one. Larger specimens are a lovely decoration in a heated conservatory or greenhouse. Younger plants should be repotted every year, older specimens only occasionally. Feed with fertilizer diluted to half strength every three weeks. Propagate by sowing spores on a peat-based compost.

137

Cyrtomium falcatum
Aspidiaceae

Fishtail Fern (137) is an ideal plant for growing indoors. It is a common fern in the forests of Asia, Africa and Polynesia, but is almost the only one of ten terrestrial species of Cyrtomium to be grown as a house plant. Because it tolerates even very low temperatures it may be grown outdoors in winter — in a sheltered position and provided with a protective covering. The arching leaves, up to 50 cm (20 in) long, composed of leathery, pointed, glossy leaflets, are very attractive.

It does well in a mixture of peat, leaf mould, rotted turves and sand. Feed about once a month from spring until autumn. Propagate by dividing the rhizomes of mature plants or by sowing the spores on a peat compost.

Phlebodium aureum
Polypodiaceae

This species (138) is native to the tropical regions of South America. Its leaves, up to 1 m (39 in) long, are deeply divided, coated with a bluish bloom, entirely glabrous and with stiff stalks. The specific name is derived from the golden-yellow colour of the sori, which are scattered over the entire undersurface of the leaves.

A good growing medium is a clay-peat compost. This fern does not require extra humidity or misting, but water regularly and do not let the compost dry out. It does best in partial shade; direct sun and full shade are equally detrimental. It does well at

139

normal room temperature but do not let·the temperature fall below 12°C (54°F) in winter. Propagate by planting spores or by dividing the rhizomes. Pieces as small as 2 cm (¾ in) soon produce young shoots at a temperature of about 20°C (68°F).

Asplenium nidus
Aspleniaceae

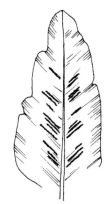

detail showing the tip of
a leaf

Bird's Nest Fern (139) grows epiphytically on the trunks of trees in the forests of tropical Asia and Polynesia. The undivided leaves, which may be more than 1 m (39 in) long, are arranged to form a kind of funnel or nest (Latin _nidus_ means nest). This enables it to catch humus and rainwater and direct them straight to the roots. The sori are clustered on the underside along the lateral veins, appearing to the casual glance like brownish-black parallel stripes.

This fern does well indoors. It requires a temperature of 20°-25°C (68°-77°F); the winter temperature should not fall below 18°C (64°F). Direct sunlight is harmful. Suitable compost is a mixture of leaf mould, peat and sand, with a pH of 5. Water liberally and mist regularly to maintain humidity at a level of at least 60 per cent. Propagate by sowing spores. They will soon germinate at a temperature of 22°C (72°F). Asplenium is very attractive if grown on an epiphyte stump in imitation of its natural habitat.

140

141

Selaginella apoda
(syn. *S. apus*)
Selaginellaceae

This species (140), native to North America, is a low-growing plant that rapidly spreads to form a yellow-green carpet. It is often used as underplanting in the greenhouse.

It cannot be grown indoors in pots because the level of humidity would be too low for healthy growth, but it does well in a miniature conservatory, plant-case or bottle garden. It does well in cool conditions and should never be exposed to direct sunlight.

Selaginella pallescens
(syn. *S. emmeliana*)
Selaginellaceae

This Selaginella (141), native to Mexico, has upright branches reaching a length of 30 cm (12 in). The leaves are terminated by a spiny point; the lateral leaves are larger than those growing in the centre of the stem. It requires constantly moist, but not sodden, compost. It does well indoors. Another species well-known even to amateurs is *S. lepidophylla*, native to the dry regions of California and Mexico. Its stems curl into a tight brownish ball in dry conditions. When moisture is provided, by putting it in a dish with water, for example, it 'comes to life' by unfurling into a green rosette. This property, called hydrochasia, is retained by the plants for several years.

GROWING UNDER GLASS

It would be difficult, and undesirable, to turn a flat or house into a greenhouse, but a miniature conservatory or glass plant-case can be built quite easily. At the very least, large glass containers such as a demijohn, fishbowl or giant brandy goblet can take the place of a greenhouse on a small scale. They can provide an ideal environment for growing plants with special requirements.

First and foremost, such glass containers provide high levels of humidity which are easy to regulate and maintain. The plants can be misted very conveniently without any fear that the water will drip on furniture or carpets.

A miniature conservatory has plenty of light because it is constructed beside a window. A glass plant-case, unless it is positioned close to a window, may require additional, artificial lighting. Light is not merely vital to plant growth, but is also an aesthetic consideration, for it heightens the beauty of the plants' colours. The intensity of the light varies in different parts of the container and you should keep this in mind when putting the plants in place. Plants with variegated foliage or brightly coloured flowers should be put in the dimmer parts of the container, while plants with less vivid coloration should be put where the light is brightest.

Plant-cases and miniature conservatories can be heated, and the temperature inside regulated as required. This makes it possible to grow even very delicate plants, such as aroids, bromeliads and many carnivorous species.

Demijohns, bottle gardens and fishbowls are neither heated nor provided with additional light. They should be placed close to a window, but not in direct sunlight which causes excessive condensation on the inside of the glass.

143

Miniature
conservatory (142)

Episcia cupreata
Gesneriaceae

This South American plant (143), native to the forests of Colombia, makes numerous runners at the nodes that root readily; the stem is very short. The leaves are deeply wrinkled, hairy, crenate on the margins and extremely variegated. The solitary flowers are very conspicuous.

It is very suitable for growing in arrangements with other plants in dishes or hanging baskets. It also grows well on an epiphyte stump in a plant-case or terrarium. Its small size makes it a good choice for a bottle garden. It requires quite a high temperature; in winter, it must not fall below 18°C (64°F). A fairly humid atmosphere is essential. Propagate by means of the runners or by tip cuttings.

Fittonia verschaffeltii
Acanthaceae

Mosaic Plant (144, 145). The genus Fittonia has only two species. Their natural range extends from Colombia to Peru. The leaves of Fittonias are opposite and ovate with blunt tips. They are coloured dark green with a network of crimson veins. The cultivar 'Argyroneura' (144) has white veins. The cultivar 'Nana' (145) is a very low-growing form. The decorative, sulphur-

144

145

yellow flowers, with a narrow tube opening out into two lips, are arranged in terminal spikes.

They require a warm environment and very humid atmosphere. They do not tolerate draught. They are, therefore, ideal plants for growing in a glassed enclosure. They are often grown in heated greenhouses, where they are used to form a lovely, thick, colourful underplanting. They do best in bottle gardens and fishbowls, but can also be grown in a shallow dish, where their prostrate, richly branching stems are displayed to good advantage. Fittonias are not in the least demanding in terms of light, and the leaves retain their lovely coloration even in shade. Propagate by tip cuttings and by sideshoots.

Strelitzia reginae
Musaceae

Bird of Paradise Flower, Crane Plant (146). The South African genus Strelitzia has only four species. Only one is commonly grown as a house plant, although the others may very occasionally be encountered in a heated greenhouse. The flowers are reminiscent of an exotic bird. Both their colour and their shape are unusual. A sharply pointed, shuttle-like organ, consisting of fused bracts, grows sideways from the end of the thick stem. From these emerge the showy flowers with orange outer seg-

146

ments and blue inner segments. The long-stalked leaves and the flower stems are 1-2 m (39-79 in) long. The plant bears a strong similarity to a banana tree, to which it is, in fact, related.

It requires very nourishing compost and a large container; plant in open ground in a greenhouse. Maintain a high temperature and high humidity in summer; water liberally. It requires cool conditions in winter. The flowers will last a remarkably long time in a vase.

148

Eichhornia crassipes
Pontederiaceae

longitudinal and cross
section of the leaf stalk

Water Hyacinth (147) is an aquatic plant which either floats on the water's surface or roots in the muddy bottom. It is native to tropical South America but has spread to every continent. Its method of flotation is intriguing. Large intercellular spaces in the swollen leaf stalks are filled with air, so the plant is less dense and able to stay afloat. The large, pale violet flowers are very attractive.

It requires lots of light. This is not a problem in summer, but in winter it is necessary to provide artificial illumination. Alternatively, take the plant out of the water, lay it loosely on mud in a shallow dish and keep the dish in a light cool place at a temperature of 5°-10°C (41°-50°F). In summer it may be transferred to a garden pool.

Calathea makoyana
Marantaceae

The Peacock Plant (148) occurs naturally in the undergrowth of the tropical forests of Brazil. It grows from a thick rhizome and reaches a height of 30-50 cm (12-20 in). The pale green or grey-green leaves are long-stalked and the leaf blades may be up to 20 cm (8 in) long. The most striking features are the olive-green blotches on either side of the midrib and the way the veins curve from the midrib towards the margins. The underside of the leaves is purplish-red, blotched like the upper surface.

This very decorative plant is well suited to modern houses which are generally warm. It must be misted frequently or grown in a glassed enclosure to ensure adequate humidity. Otherwise, the leaf margins begin to turn brown.

Calathea ornata
Marantaceae

This species (149), like most of the genus Calathea, which includes some 100 species, has very decorative foliage. Thriving specimens may reach a height of 80- 90 cm (31-35 in). The long-stalked leaves are 30-60 cm (12-24 in) long, bright green above and red beneath. Young leaves have narrow, pinkish-red stripes between the veins. These fade to a silvery white colour in older plants. If grown in a suitable environment, this Calathea will provide further delight by bearing spikes of white flowers about 8 cm (3 in) long.

The rules for cultivation are virtually the same for all Calatheas. The plant requires a fairly high temperature, a sufficiently humid atmosphere, and an acid compost rich in humus, such as a mixture of peat and beech leaves. Do not allow the

149

compost to dry out. Ventilation is beneficial. You must be patient to begin with, for it takes quite a long time for the plants to become established. However, once they are established, growth is very rapid. Propagate by dividing the clumps.

Calathea stromata
Marantaceae

This species (150) is native to the virgin forests of Brazil where it occurs in the undergrowth. The taller plants of its natural habitat provide shade and shelter from drying winds. The frequent rains and mists at high elevations provide it with a very humid atmosphere. It forms thick clumps of stiff, long-stalked, broadly elongate leaves 10-12 cm (4-5 in) long.

It does best in a coarse, free-draining and nourishing compost. Experienced growers use a mixture of leaf mould, heath mould, peat and charcoal. A loam and peat soil is also suitable. It requires a temperature of 18°-20°C (64°-68°F) in the daytime and about 16°C (61°F) at night during the growth period. The minimum temperature is 16°C (61°F). It may be grown in shallow containers.

150

151

Cissus discolor
Vitaceae

This species (151), unlike most members of the genus Cissus, likes warm and humid conditions and lots of light. Therefore, it is best grown in a glassed enclosure. It is a rapidly growing liana with red stems, tendrils and stalks. The velvety leaf blades are 15 cm (10 in) long, 8 cm (3 in) wide. They are marbled above and coloured reddish-purple on the underside. Small clusters of yellow flowers grow from the axils of the leaves.

To ensure that the leaves are as colourful as possible, provide

169

plenty of light. Never allow the compost to dry out because the leaves will drop. Propagate by tip cuttings.

Calathea picturata
'Argentea'
Marantaceae

This cultivar (152) has white leaves with green only on the margin. The type species, native to Brazil, has dark green leaves with a single, broad white band along the midrib and another, narrower band along the margin. It is purplish-red on the under-surface.

Like most plants that grow in tropical forests, it does not tolerate direct sunlight. It requires a high temperature in summer; do not allow the winter temperature to fall below 18°C (64°F). It needs a high level of humidity; the relative humidity should be 60—70 per cent. Propagate by dividing the clumps.

Calathea zebrina
Marantaceae

This perennial herb (153), native to Brazil, has long-stalked, lanceolate leaves which are pointed at the tip and at the base. They are glabrous and dark green above, except for the pale green primary and secondary veins, and purplish-red on the underside. The short, thick inflorescence is composed of white and violet flowers with striking violet bracts. Conditions for growing are the same as for _C. picturata_ (see above).

170

Pinguicula gypsicola
Lentibulariaceae

This species (154) is native to Mexico, where it grows on the northern and northeastern slopes of mountains. The summer rosettes are composed of extremely narrow, linear leaves, whereas the leaves of the small, button-like winter rosettes are flat and rather broad. There are numerous glands on the upper side of the leaves. The flowers are large with a narrow spur about 2.5 cm (1 in) long.

Cultivation is quite easy. It requires a fairly high summer temperature and liberal watering. In winter it requires a moderately warm location, plenty of light and high humidity. Propagate by sowing seeds on the surface of coarse, wet peat (they germinate in light). Do not store seeds as they quickly lose the ability to germinate. Vegetative propagation by dividing the clumps is a more rapid method. New plants may also be obtained from the leaves, but use only undamaged ones.

Pinguicula moranensis
Lentibulariaceae

This insectivorous plant (155) has striking, undivided fleshy leaves. The inflorscence is usually 5-15 cm (2-6 in) high and composed of yellow, purple or violet flowers with petals flared at the end and a long spur. The fruit is a many-seeded capsule.

153

171

154

Pinguicula moranensis—vegetative propagation by means of a leaf

The leaf blades serve to trap insects; their upper surfaces are thickly covered with stalked glands which secrete a sticky fluid to catch insects. In addition, sessile glands produce a mucilaginous secretion containing enzymes which digest the bodies of the captured insects. The leaves of some species furl on the margins to envelop the victim.

Pinguiculas grow in stony places, around springs, on sweating rocks, in peat meadows and on moors where the soil tends to be damp and poor in nitrogen and other elements. They are usually found in very humid locations. *P. moranensis* has a thick rosette of glossy leaves (the sheen is produced by the numerous glands) and flowers about 5 cm (2 in) across. The petals are narrow and do not touch each other. In this they differ from those of the similar species *P. colimensis*. The spur is three to four times longer than the corolla tube. *P. moranensis* stands up well to poor light and in winter it does not require cooler conditions.

Nepenthes—hybr.
Nepenthaceae

Members of the genus Nepenthes (156) are insectivorous plants with a special organ shaped like a pitcher for catching insects. The edge and inner sides of the pitcher are covered with glands which secrete a liquid that attracts insects. It has a lid and a smooth, swollen edge down which the victim readily slides. Once inside it is unable to get out. In the bottom of the pitcher is an acid liquid containing pepsin, an enzyme that digests the insect body. The pitchers of the illustrated species, which may be up to 30 cm (12 in) long, are yellow-green in colour. The lower part is spotted red and the edge is coloured chestnut brown. Nepenthes includes about 70 species. Hybrid species are most commonly grown because they are hardier and often more decorative than the type species.

For good growth, the plants require light, but not direct sunlight, the whole year, as well as high humidity and plenty of fresh air. The heat requirements differ according to the species. The most suitable growing medium is a mixture of polypodium roots, sphagnum moss, coarse leaf mould, crushed bark, sand and charcoal.

Sarracenia rubra
Sarraceniaceae

This insectivorous plant (157) has very distinctive leaves. They are tubular or pitcher-like, with a wing-like strip on the side facing inwards towards the centre of the rosette. Glandular hairs

Pitchers of various
species of the genus
Nepenthes

156

inside secrete enzymes that digest the bodies of captured insects. The leaf 'pitchers' are terminated by a kind of lid at the top. The drooping flowers, measuring up to 8 cm (3 in) long, grow singly on a long stiff stalk. They have a violet-like scent. The five-sepalled calyx is persistent, the corolla is composed of five petals that drop. The style is shaped like an umbrella. There are eight species in the genus Sarracenia, distributed throughout the Atlantic region of North America.

S. rubra requires a light and well ventilated position. Provide cool conditions in winter. The best growing medium is a mixture of fresh sphagnum moss, peat, sand and charcoal. Water and mist the plant regularly.

Sarracenia purpurea
Sarraceniaceae

Northern Pitcher Plant (158) is native to the Atlantic coast of North America. It grows in boggy places and on the wet shores of stagnant water. Its distribution extends to the Great Lakes. The leaves are 15-45 cm (6-8 in) long, and up to 10 cm (4 in) thick in the middle. They have broad wing-like stripes. The petals are purplish-red and drop along with the stamens within 14 days after the flower has opened. The flower then straightens and remains upright until the autumn.

Species vary considerably in their heat requirements; it is important to bear native habitats in mind. *S. purpurea* is hardy and tolerates a light frost in winter. It can, in fact, be grown outdoors and will often become established. In summer it needs to

157

158

be shaded. Sarracenias are generally propagated by vegetative means; divide clumps of plants and rhizomes. When propagating by means of seeds, sow them as soon as they are ripe, for they remain viable for only a short time. Sow them on the surface of moist sphagnum moss in a flat dish and cover the dish with glass. As soon as the seedlings are about 2 cm (¾ in) high, prick them out into the growing medium.

Dionaea muscipula
Droseraceae

Venus Fly-trap (159) was the first commonly grown insectivorous house plant. It is also the only terrestrial plant that captures insects by snapping shut the leaves. The leaves form a rosette about 7-15 cm (2¾-6 in) in diameter. The leaf stalks are broadened, wing-like and the basal, underground part forms a kind of tuber in which reserves of food are stored. The leaf blade forms the trap proper; it is less than 3 cm (1 in) long, rounded in outline with long, stiff hairs on the margin. The two halves of the blade can snap shut with lightning speed, imprisoning the insect inside. The inner side of the leaf blade is often reddish and covered near the margin with nectary glands

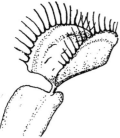

Dionaea muscipula
—open fly trap

that attract insects, and minute glands that secrete a digestive juice. Venus Fly-trap is capable of capturing insects up to 3 cm (1 in) long. After snapping shut, the leaf remains closed for several days. The flowers, up to 2 cm (¾ in) across, have five white petals that do not fall; they wilt and remain on the flower stalks.

In winter, the plant requires cool conditions, about 5°C (41°F). Apply water sparingly in winter, but do not let the compost dry out. Use soft water. The relative humidity should be almost 70 per cent.

Drosera spathulata
Droseraceae

This species (160) is one of 85 in the genus Drosera. The sundew family has only four genera: Drosophyllum, Dionaea, Al-

159

drovanda and Drosera. The first three genera have only one species each. They are distributed mostly in the southern hemisphere; three are found in Europe. Droseras are small perennial herbs. They usually have a ground rosette of leaves thickly covered with glandular hairs (tentacles) secreting a sticky liquid that glitters in the sun. This is why they were given the genus name (the Greek *drosero* means covered with dew). The flowers are white. *D. spathulata* forms a rosette of spatulate leaves which grows tightly against the ground and is thickly covered with red tentacles. The upright inflorescences are composed of about 15 flowers.

Droseras require lots of sun, fresh air and very moist compost. They grow well in fresh sphagnum moss or on peat. Propagate by means of seeds sown on peat in a flat dish (merely pressed in) and covered with glass.

Rhipsalis cassutha
Cactaceae

Mistletoe Cactus (161) belongs to the cactus family, but this plant shows little resemblance to the typical cactus. It is an epiphyte with rounded, trailing stems. The white globose fruits resemble the berries of mistletoe (this gives it its common name).

160

178

161

It is found throughout the tropical regions of the Americas, in Africa and Sri Lanka, where a further 60 species also grow.

Growing it indoors is quite difficult. It requires lots of light, but not direct sunlight, and fairly humid atmosphere. A good growing medium is a mixture of equal parts of leaf mould, sphagnum moss and sand. Stem cuttings root readily at a temperature of 25°C (77°F) and at a high level of humidity. Cuttings with aerial roots are particularly good for propagation. The plant is also readily propagated from seed.

Pellionia repens
Urticaceae

This species (162) and *P. pulchra* are the only two of some 50 species of Pellionia grown as house plants. *P. repens*, a tropical species from southeast Asia, has prostrate stems pressed close

to the ground and alternate, two-ranked, sessile leaves that are
3-5 cm (1-2 in) long and 2-3 cm (¾-1 in) wide. Because they are
small plants they are well suited to small glass containers or flat
dishes. Never allow the compost to dry out. Propagate by means
of stem cuttings. To root they require a temperature of 22°-24°C
(72°-75°F). After they have become established the young
plants should be pruned several times to make bushy growth.

**Caladium-Bicolor
—hybr.**
(syn. *C.× hortulanum*)
Araceae

This (163) is a hybrid developed by crossing several species
(C. bicolor, C. picturatum and *C. schonburgkii).* The leaves of cal-
adiums are among the loveliest in the whole plant kingdom.
A disadvantage is that the plants have a distinct period of rest

163

from autumn until spring. During this time the leaves drop and the plants die back.

The plant is quite demanding in terms of heat and humidity. The optimum temperature is 25°-30°C (77°-86°F) and it should not drop below 20°C (68°F). The atmosphere should be so humid that water condenses on the leaves. In winter, when the plant is resting, the tubers should be left in the compost without watering or else stored in a dry place. In early March they should then be put in a mixture of frame soil, peat and sand, moved to a warm place and watered liberally.

Alocasia lowii
Araceae

This tropical plant (164) grows in the forests of Borneo. It has very decorative, sagittate, leathery leaves. They are coloured olive-green with prominent white stripes along the veins and a light band edging the margin; the underside is purplish-red.

It stands up well to partial shade and even tolerates full shade. However, it is demanding in terms of heat; it requires a summer temperature of up to 25°C (77°F). In winter, the temperature should not fall below 18°C (64°F). Propagate by dividing the rhizomes.

Alocasia metallica
(syn. *A. cuprea*)
Araceae

There are about 70 species of Alocasia distributed in Asia, Malaysia and New Guinea. They have been an ornamental feature of heated greenhouses for decades. They can be grown indoors in a plant-case or terrarium where they are provided with a more humid atmosphere and higher temperature. *A. metallica* (165) has a tuberous underground rhizome from which grows a short stem bearing large sagittate leaves. The leaf stalks and the leaf blades measure up to 30 cm (12 in). They are a coppery-green above and violet on the underside. The requirements for growing *A. metallica* are the same as for *A. lowii* (see above).

Cryptanthus
bromelioides
'Tricolor'
Bromeliaceae

Cryptanthuses (166) are rather small, terrestrial plants native to eastern Brazil. Because they readily put forth tillers, they often form spreading carpets in dry forests. The generic name comes from Greek origin (*kryptos*=hidden, *anthos*=flower) and accurately describes the short-stalked flowers concealed in the leaf

165

165

rosette. The leaves have conspicuously crooked, spiny margins, and the under-surface is scaly. They are often strikingly coloured.

The lovely coloration of the foliage and its low-growing habit make the plant an ideal subject for a miniature conservatory, a plant-case or other glass containers. It does best in a light to partially shaded position, tolerating direct sun only in winter. It requires quite a high temperature, which even in winter must not fall below 18°C (64°F). A suitable growing medium is a loam and peat substrate with an admixture of sphagnum moss. Water liberally and maintain a high level of humidity. Allowing the compost to dry out occasionally will not harm the plant but it will slow its growth. Feed very occasionally with a weak solution of compound mineral fertilizer. Young plantlets are produced in large numbers in the leaf axils. These plantlets are an easy means of propagating the plant; simply cut or tear them off.

The type is about 20-40 cm (8-16 in) high. It produces large numbers of sideshoots which can be used for propagation. The leaves are faintly wavy, finely and densely toothed. They are green above and a whitish colour on the underside. The white flowers, which are about 4 cm (1½ in) long, are arranged in fairly thick clusters.

Cryptanthus bivittatus
Bromeliaceae

This species (167, 168) forms rather small, flat leaf rosettes. The leaves are very distinctive, serve as a ready means of identification, and gave rise to the plant's specific name (Latin *bi*=two,

166

167

vittatus = striped), for there are two very prominent pale stripes on the upper side. The leaves are about 20 cm (8 in) long, only slightly wavy and finely toothed on the margin, glabrous above and faintly scaly on the underside.

It is interesting to note that earlier botanists found it difficult to determine the appropriate genus of this species. Some classed it in the genus Bilbergia, others in the genus Tillandsia, and still others in the genus Nidularium.

The cultivar 'It' (167) is probably a mutant from hybrids whose parentage probably included *C. bivittatus*. It has a rosette of linear leaves about 45 cm (18 in) long and 4 cm (1½ in) wide. They are olive-green with broad, white, longitudinal stripes, and tinged bright pinkish-red on the margins and at the base. The lighter the plant's location, the more pronounced are the stripes.

Cryptanthus acaulis
Bromeliaceae

This species (169) has low, flat rosettes. The leaves, about 13 cm (5 in) long and 3 cm (1 in) wide, have long spines on the margins and are recurved at the tip. The upper side is pale green; the underside is greyish-white and covered with numerous scale-like hairs. The cultivar 'Ruber' has reddish-brown leaves.

Guzmania lingulata 'Mayor'
Bromeliaceae

Guzmanias (170) are tropical plants native to the northwestern part of South America. A few species grow in Florida and Central America. Of the 100-120 species, most are epiphytes; only some are terrestrial. The leaves are always undivided and form a funnel-shaped rosette. The flowers are in panicles or in com-

168

169

pact flowerheads. The leaf rosette of *G. lingulata* may measure up to 70 cm (27½ in) in diameter. The inflorescence is about 30 cm (12 in) long with numerous tongue-shaped bracts (hence the specific name), coloured bright red and recurved. It may contain as many as 50 white to yellow flowers; the petals are tear-shaped.

Guzmanias require a temperature of about 25°C (77°F). Even in winter it must not fall below 18°C (64°F). They prefer partial shade. They have very demanding humidity requirements — water may be allowed to collect inside the leaf rosette but must be poured off occasionally. However, they do not tolerate soggy compost. They are propagated on a large scale by nurserymen. New plants are generally obtained from seed, for vegetative propagation of Guzmanias by means of sideshoots is relatively rare.

Guzmania sanguinea
Bromeliaceae

This species (171) grows in Central and South America as an epiphyte. It has a low stem from which grows a flat, funnel-shaped rosette of stiff leaves. These are an attractive feature for they turn vivid red and yellow before the flowers appear. The central leaves are markedly shorter than the outside ones. The

187

inflorescence does not protrude from the leaf rosette, but is concealed inside the funnel. There are usually seven to twelve yellow flowers about 6 cm (2½ in) long. *G. sanguinea* is the only species in the genus that tolerates direct sun and a rather dry atmosphere. It does well in a warm room if correctly watered.

Guzmania zahnii
Bromeliaceae

This species (172) was named after the botanist Zahn, who collected plants in Central America. The type species grows in the forests of Costa Rica and has yielded a great many cultivars. Like other species of this genus, the leaves are arranged in large, funnel-shaped rosettes. They can be up to 60 cm (24 in) long, but are only 23-35 mm ($^9/_{10}$-1$^2/_5$ in) wide. They are brownish-green. The inflorescence extends only slightly beyond the leaves and is composed of 10-15 yellow flowers about 3 cm (1 in) long. The bracts are large, flared and coloured red.

188

Nidularium lineatum
(syn. *N. innocenti*
var. *lineatum*)
Bromeliaceae

This species (173), like all Nidulariums, is native to Brazil. It grows as an epiphyte on trees. It has a rosette of leaves that may be up to 60 cm (24 in) in diameter. The leaves are stiff, leathery, pointed and spiny-toothed on the margins. They are green on the upper side and dark violet-red with numerous white stripes on the underside. The inflorescence, growing in the centre of the rosette, does not extend beyond the leaves. The brilliant red bracts protruding from the inflorescence are very striking. The petals are white with a green base. The flowers in the centre of the inflorescence open first and the marginal flowers open later. The great advantage of the blossoms of Nidulariums is their longevity; they may last as long as three months.

It is an extremely decorative house plant, especially if it is affixed to a stump in an epiphytic arrangement. Nidulariums require a relatively high temperature and slight shade, for in their natural habitat they are accustomed to the dimness of a dense forest. They tolerate a less humid atmosphere but must have water in the centre of the leaf rosette and a moist substrate. The best potting medium is a mixture of peat, sand, beech leaves and charcoal, or at least peat and sand. Good drainage, in the

171

189

form of crocks or pieces of charcoal, is essential. Putting moisture-retentive sphagnum moss around the plants is recommended.

Guzmania—hybr. 'Claudine'
Bromeliaceae

The great interest in decorative Guzmanias prompted many growers to engage in the selective breeding of less demanding species. This has resulted in the development of many different cultivars, one of which is illustrated here (174). Typical of this cultivar are the fiery red, flared bracts; the leaves are sometimes pink at the base and at the margins.

Guzmania monostachya
Bromeliaceae

This Guzmania (175) is distributed from Florida to Bolivia, growing as high up as 2,000 m (6,500 ft). The very dense rosettes reach a height of 30-40 cm (12-16 in). The leaves are 2-3 cm (^{3}/$_4$-1 in) wide, yellow-green, paler on the underside, and completely glabrous. The inflorescence overtops the leaf rosette — it is about 50 cm (20 in) high. The bracts are approximately 3 cm (1 in) long; those at the bottom of the inflorescence are brownish-red and longitudinally striped, those at the tip, where there are no flowers, are a brilliant red. The white flowers grow from the axils of the brightly coloured bracts, to which they form a striking contrast.

Because it is an epiphyte it is very attractive when grown on a stump in a plant-case. It requires light, but not direct sun, and tolerates partial shade. The compost should contain an adequate amount of peat and must be kept permanently moist. As with all bromeliads, use only soft water. It requires high relative humidity — 60 per cent is best.

Vriesia—hybr. 'Foster Favorite'
Bromeliaceae

Vriesia is a large genus. The exact number of species it contains is not known but is estimated to be 180-200. It was named in honour of the renowned Dutch professor of botany Hugo de Vries. Most Vriesias grow as epiphytes and are native to Brazil. The leaves typically form a funnel-shaped rosette and the two-ranked, compressed flower spike has striking variegated bracts. The illustrated cultivar (176) has a large rosette of very stiff leaves, about 50 cm (20 in) long and 10 cm (4 in) wide. They have irregular, reddish-brown, horizontal stripes on the underside. The erect inflorescences, composed of 20-25 flowers, are up to 1 m (39 in) long; the rachis is green dotted with reddish-brown. The flowers are pale yellow.

173

Vriesias require a high temperature, a very humid atmosphere and some shade. The usual growing medium is a loam and peat mixture with sphagnum moss. When watering, it is necessary to top up the water in the leaf funnel. Propagate by means of the side rosettes.

Vriesia hieroglyphica
Bromeliaceae

This Vriesia (177) acquired its specific name because of the dark, horizontal markings on the leaves. It is native to Brazil. The leaf rosettes are extraordinarily large, more than 1 m (39 in) across. The individual leaves are very stiff, about 50 cm (20 in) long and 10 cm (4 in) wide. The inflorescences are also big, 60-80 cm (24-32 in) long, and composed of separate spikes. The bracts, up to 3 cm (1 in) long, are yellow-green. The yellow flowers are two-ranked at first; later they bend to one side. They are about 6 cm (2½ in) long.

174

**Neoregelia carolinae
'Tricolor'**
Bromeliaceae

Blushing Bromeliad (178). The leaves are arranged in a funnel-shaped rosette. The very short inflorescence is concealed inside the funnel. The tough, leathery leaves may be up to 40 cm (16 in) long. They are truncated and shortly pointed at the tip and densely edged with minute spines on the margins. The leaves in the centre of the rosettes turn brilliant red at the onset of flowers. The others are dark green, except for those of the cultivar 'Tricolor' which are striped yellow-white and flushed with red. The type species is native to Brazil.

Neoregelias require a high temperature and ample atmospheric moisture — the relative humidity should not fall to less than 60 per cent. There must always be water in the centre of the leaf rosette. Propagate by the side rosettes.

Aechmea chantinii
Bromeliaceae

This species (179), native to the rain forests of the Amazon, was introduced into Europe in 1877. It is one of the most widely cultivated species of Aechmea. The extremely decorative rosette of tough, leathery leaves resembles a large funnel 59-60 cm (20-24 in) in diameter. The leaves are 5-6 cm (2-2^1/$_2$ in) wide, with long brown spines on the margins as well as one at the tip. The inflorescence growing from the centre of the rosette is up to 40 cm (16 in) high and has striking bright red bracts. The sepals are slightly more than 1 cm (^{2}/$_5$ in) long and coloured red with a green tip; the petals are yellow and are not nearly as eye-catching as the bracts. A great advantage is that the flowers are very long-lasting.

This Aechmea can be grown in a pot or as an epiphyte on a branch or stump. All species of Aechmea do well at normal room temperature and will tolerate higher temperatures. Do not allow the winter temperature to fall below 15°C (59°F). The plants must be provided with constant moisture. As long as there is water in the centre of the rosette it does not matter if the compost dries out by chance. If the plant is grown in a pot, the compost should be a mixture of peat, litter and sand; if it is grown as an epiphyte, its base should be wrapped in sphagnum moss to which some compost has been added. When misting the plant be sure some water remains in the centre of the rosette.

Aechmea fasciata
Bromeliaceae

The Urn Plant (180) is considered the hardiest thermophilous plant suited to indoor cultivation. In its native Brazil, it grows as an epiphyte on trees. It forms funnel-shaped rosettes of tough leaves, up to 50 cm (20 in) long and 6-10 cm (2^1/$_2$-4 in) wide. They are shortly toothed on the margins and spiny at the

177

178

tips. The greyish-silver, horizontal stripes on the leaves are formed by minute, scale-like hairs. A thick, pink stem, topped by a tightly packed inflorescence grows from the centre of the leaf rosette. The pink bracts are more striking than the flowers. The inflorescence can last for several months.

In indoor cultivation, it is usually grown on a stump or branch. However, it also does well as a pot plant. It even stands up well to unventilated, smoky rooms.

Tillandsia disticha
Bromeliaceae

Tillandsia, with 400 species, is the largest genus in the family Bromeliaceae. It was named by Linnaeus in honour of the Swedish botanist Elias Tillands (1640-93). *T. disticha* (181) grows as an epiphyte in Colombia, Ecuador and Peru. The undivided leaves are usually arranged in a rosette. They are often silvery grey because they are covered with numerous scales that absorb moisture and minute dust particles from the atmosphere. The water absorbed by the scales is passed on to the inner leaf tissues. During periods of drought, the scales are filled with air. They reflect the sun's rays and so greatly reduce the evaporation of water. The illustrated Tillandsia puts out tillers and so soon forms clumps of plants. The leaves grow to a length of about 30 cm (12 in) and are covered with greyish or brownish scales. The spikes of flowers are 4-6 cm ($1^1/_2$-$2^1/_2$ in) long, 8 mm ($^3/_{10}$ in) wide and greatly flattened. The sepals are only 8 mm ($^3/_{10}$ in), the petals 15 mm ($^3/_5$ in) long.

It is usually grown as an epiphyte indoors, generally in a plant-case. It requires plenty of air and a high temperature. A temperature of 10°-15°C (50°-59°F) is sufficient in winter. From spring to autumn, mist the plant at least twice a day. Tillandsias are propagated either by sowing seeds directly on rough bark or by detaching daughter plants. *T. disticha* can be

179

180

easily propagated by means of the tillers. The majority of species are grown as epiphytes.

Tillandsia filifolia
Bromeliaceae

The specific name of this Tillandsia (182) describes the thin, grey, thread-like leaves which are spread out to all sides. The colour is due to numerous scales. Small bulbs at the base of the plant serve as reservoirs of water. Each plant produces several flower spikes.

It requires a very humid atmosphere and does best on an epiphyte stump in a glassed enclosure.

Tillandsia cyanea
Bromeliaceae

This species (183) can be grown as a potted plant, a rarity among Tillandsias. It grows in the rain forests of Ecuador at elevations of 600-1,000 m (2,000-3,300 ft). It belongs to the group of 'cistern' Tillandsias that resemble Vriesias. The leaves, arranged in a rosette, form a funnel to catch rainwater that collects in the 'cup' at the base. Water is also absorbed through the numerous roots. The leaf rosette may be up to 40 cm (16 in)

198

across. The leaf blades are only slightly scaly. The bracts of the inflorescence are green to pinkish red, the corollas blue-violet.

It requires a light peaty soil, a small amount of which must be provided for the plant even if it is grown as an epiphyte on a branch.

Tillandsia plumosa
Bromeliaceae

This plant (184) is native to Mexico where it grows only north of Oaxaca. It is an epiphyte found at elevations as high as 3,000 m (9,800 ft). Because the numerous, outward-spreading scales on the leaves make them look as if they were feathered, this Tillandsia was given the specific name *plumosa* (Latin *pluma* = feather). The inflorescence extends beyond the leaves.

It requires a very sunny and light position, and only very little water.

Tillandsia usneoides
Bromeliaceae

The species' (185, 186) natural range of distribution extends from the southern USA through Central America to Argentina and Chile. In arid regions the plants are silvery grey; in regions with greater rainfall they are greenish. They grow on all sorts of objects — the branches of trees, telegraph poles, fences, walls, other plants and rocks. The long, trailing stems like tufts of hair do not in the least look as if they belonged to a bromeliad. The plant looks much more like a lichen of the genus Usnea (hence its specific name). It has no roots. The only rootlet appears during germination and then disappears, its function being to an-

181   182

184

chor the seed to the substrate. The weak stems, about 1 mm (1/50 in) thick, may be extremely long; in their native habitats they may measure as much as 8 m (26 ft). Both the stems and the leaves are coloured silvery grey. The yellow-green flowers are borne singly on stems growing from the axils of the bracts.

Propagate either from seed (less common) or by vegetative means. In their natural habitat vegetative reproduction is very easy for the plants are torn apart and carried to other places by the wind. *T. usneoides* is an aerophytic plant, that is, one that does not make roots but absorbs water from the air.

Tillandsia tectorum
Bromeliaceae

This plant (187) is quite common in southern Ecuador and central Peru, where it forms thick, spreading masses in the mountains, often between areas of rock. The specific name *tectorum* is Latin, meaning 'of rooftops' (in this case 'of rocks').

T. tectorum grows at the same altitude as cacti, so the same growing conditions are recommended for both house plants. It requires a light and sunny position. Water sparingly. Otherwise it is an absolutely undemanding plant; it need not even be put in compost.

201

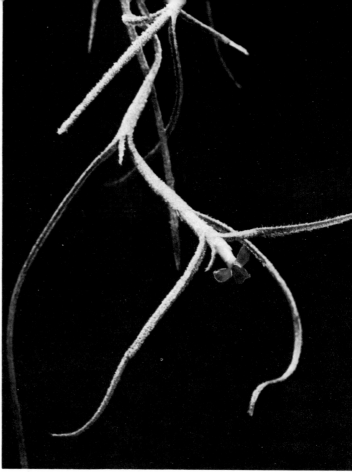

185   186

Tillandsia ionantha
Bromeliaceae

This species (188) is native to Mexico, Guatemala, Nicaragua and Honduras. It grows at elevations as high as 1,300 m (4,300 ft). It forms large tufts or cushions of curving, awl-shaped leaves that turn red during the flowering period. The petals, up to 4 cm (1½ in) long, are white tipped with violet-blue. This is a very variable species.

It requires a moist environment and lots of light and sun. In summer it may even be grown outdoors.

Codiaeum variegatum var. pictum
Euphorbiaceae

Although the genus Codiaeum has 14 species distributed throughout Malaysia and on Pacific islands, only one is grown as an ornamental plant. It is often grown in pots and can be found in almost every heated greenhouse. Croton (189, 190) is a shrub that may attain a height of 2 m (79 in). The leathery, evergreen leaves may be ovate or variously lobed, sometimes very narrow to linear. Their coloration is also variable — green combined with yellow, orange, red or violet. The flowers are inconspicuous. The cultivar 'Norma' (189) has very narrow leaves

Codiaeum variegatum
—variability of the leaves

clustered in tufts on the stems. The markings on the leaf blades are irregular, each blotch being of a different size and shape. Another exceptionally lovely cultivar is 'Golden Star' (190). It has broadly ovate leaves with long-pointed tips, and lovely golden-yellow markings.

Crotons require a very light position sheltered from direct sunlight. They tolerate sun without damage only in winter. Crotons need a high temperature; the optimum temperature in winter is about 20°C (68°F); in summer it should be much higher. At low temperatures, the leaves begin to drop. The relative humidity must not be less than 60 per cent. Water liberally and mist the plants regularly, even in winter. Because they do not tolerate draughts the room should not be aired too much. The best growing medium is a mixture of two parts leaf mould, one part frame soil, and one part each of peat and sand. Put a drainage layer at the bottom of the container. Repot young plants every year; older plants every two or three years. Prune the plants to promote bushy growth. Propagate by air layering.

Pilea cadierei
Urticaceae

The Aluminium Plant (191) is native to the tropical forests of Asia. It was discovered at the relatively late date of 1938, in Vietnam. Although its flowers are not striking, it has very attractive foliage. The leaves have three prominent veins and are marked with silvery patches, hence the common name.

187

188

189

Because it grows in the bottom layer of tropical mountain forests it does not require much light; it must be protected from direct sunlight. It requires a mixture of two parts frame soil, two parts leaf mould and one part sand or a loam and peat compost. The temperature should be about 27°C (77°F). Water regularly and maintain a relative humidity of no less than 60 per cent at all times. Feed with a solution of compound mineral fertilizer once a week.

Pilea spruceana
Urticaceae

This (192, 193) is one of 200 species of the genus Pilea distributed in tropical regions throughout the world. _P. spruceana_ is native to Peru and Venezuela. It makes numerous runners with ascending stems about 10 cm (4 in) long. The leaves are hairy and covered with blister-like growths. They are light green which, in very young plants, is often flushed with red.

The cultivar 'Norfolk' (193) has almost orbicular leaves coloured a striking bronze-brown, sometimes even red, with large white patches between the veins. It is a very decorative plant but must be provided with a fairly high temperature and a humid atmosphere.

Pilea crassifolia
Urticaceae

This plant (194) is better known as *P. mollis* or as 'Moon Valley'. It is certainly the most decorative species of the entire genus. Its most ornamental features are the leaves, which are very wrinkled, pointed-ovate and with crenate margins.

Protect it from direct sunlight. It requires a temperature of 20°-25°C (68°-77°F) in summer and 18°C (64°F) in winter. Water and mist it regularly.

Columnea minor
Gesneriaceae

Columneas (195) are native to tropical America and most grow as epiphytes. Even though there are 100-120 species of Columneas, only very few 'pure' species are cultivated. Hybrids are more popular. They are usually hardier and often have more striking features, such as larger flowers, than the type. They are among the loveliest of plants for hanging containers, for the trailing stems with numerous flowers are exceptionally attractive in such an arrangement. *C. minor* is native to Ecuador. It has longish-ovate, hairy leaves. Single tubular flowers, thickly

190

covered with carmine-red hairs, grow from the leaf axils. They are produced over a period of nearly four months.

It requires a light position, but not in direct sun. It grows best at a temperature of 20°C (68°F), but in summer it will tolerate

193

even 30°C (86°F). In winter the temperature should be about 18°C (64°F). It requires a very high level of humidity but should be watered only in moderation. Too much water causes the leaves to drop. Feed during the growth period with organic fertilizer. Propagate by means of stem cuttings, taken with two pairs of leaves, or by means of seeds.

Hypoestes phyllostachya
(syn. *H. sanguinolenta*)
Acanthaceae

This (196) is a sub-shrub from Madagascar. There are about 40 species of Hypoestes distributed in Madagascar and South Africa. In its natural habitat, *H. phyllostachya* reaches a height of 1 m (39 in). Grown as a house plant, however, it is much shorter. It is cultivated chiefly for its leaves, which are patterned with prominent red veins and pink patches. The flowers are not particularly striking; they are pale blue-violet and grow singly from the axils of the leaves.

It requires a high level of humidity — 60 per cent. It needs a very light position. When supplied with sufficient light, the leaves are beautifully coloured. It is readily propagated by tip cuttings which should be cut back after they have rooted to promote branching. It can also be propagated from seed.

207

Siderasis fuscata
Commelinaceae

Brown Spiderwort (197) is native to Brazil. Many members of the family Commelinaceae are succulent perennial herbs, others are perennial herbs without succulent leaves, and still others are annuals. A typical feature of all the genera are 3-merous flowers growing from the axils of the leaves; the fruit is a capsule. Their natural range of distribution is in the tropics and sub-tropics. However the delimitation of the individual genera of the family is not simple, and botanists concerned with the study of this family differ markedly in their opinions. Siderasis is one of the small genera. *S. fuscata* forms compact rosettes of broadly ovate, generally bluntly-tipped leaves. A white stripe along the midrib makes an attractive contrast with the olive-green of the upper surface. The leaves are completely covered with brownish-red hairs.

It requires quite a high temperature. Regular watering and misting are essential for good growth. Propagate by means of stem cuttings.

194

195

Sonerila margaritacea This (198) is one of 70 species of Sonerila distributed from
Melastomataceae India to China and southward to Indonesia. A low-growing
sub-shrub, it reaches a height of only 30 cm (12 in) in the wild
and even less in cultivation. The leaves are broadly ovate, dark
green with silvery white patches and minute dots on the upper
surface and pale green flushed with red on the underside. The
inflorescence is an umbel composed of about ten pink flowers.

It is a warmth-loving plant that requires a temperature of 20°-
25°C (68°-77°F) throughout the year. It needs a light position.

196

197

198

Gloriosa
rothschildiana
Liliaceae

the tubers

High humidity — 70 per cent — is essential. It grows well in a bottle garden or terrarium. Water regularly. When watering, take care not to make the leaves wet. Propagate by means of stem cuttings.

Glory Lily (199) is a liana native to tropical Africa. It has glossy, opposite leaves, sometimes in whorls of three, and terminated by tendrils with which the plant clings to a support. The flowers, 10-15 cm (4-6 in) across, grow singly on very thin stalks. The long style is geniculate, the stigma three-branched. It produces cylindrical tubers, 15 cm (6 in) long. They are poisonous, containing the alkaloid colchicine.

The plant dies back in winter, so limit watering in the autumn and withhold it completely in the winter. Water liberally during the growing period and feed with organic fertilizers. The flowers are good for cutting and will last up to 10 days in a vase. Propagate by means of the tubers. Place them horizontally in the pot. A supporting grid should be put in the pot at the same

211

199

time as the tubers so as not to damage them by later insertion when they have started new growth. As soon as young plants appear they should be put in a very light place. The tubers should be overwintered at a temperature of 8°-10°C (46°-50°F).

Anthurium
warocqueanum
Araceae

This Anthurium (200) is native to Colombia. It is a member of a South American genus that numbers some 600 species. Only a few have become popular house plants, including *A. scherze-rianum* and *A. andreanum* (see p. 250-51). These, however, underwent such extensive cross-breeding that there are now innumerable cultivated forms but the original type species are no longer known. The most striking feature of *A. warocqueanum* is the foliage. The leaf stalks are up to 80 cm (32 in) long and the leaf blades up to 1 m (39 in) long. They have silvery-white veins and hang downwards. The greenish spathe is crooked, 10 cm (4 in) long and relatively narrow — less than 2 cm (¾ in). The spadix is short-stalked.

It requires very nourishing and free-draining compost. It needs diffused light. The temperature in winter should be 16°-18°C (61°-64°F) and at least 22°C (72°F) during the rest of the year. Propagate by dividing the clumps at any time of the year, except November and December, or by sowing seeds.

212

Acorus gramineus
'Variegatus'
Araceae

Sweet Flag (201) has been incorrectly offered for sale as an aquarium plant, but it does not tolerate permanent submersion. It is a grass-like perennial herb, forming thick clumps of linear

200

leaves, usually 15-20 cm (6-8 in) long. They are usually dark green but those of the cultivar 'Variegatus' are striped green and yellow. The small spadices are composed of minute flowers.

It does best in a light position, but tolerates partial shade. It should not be exposed to direct sun. Because it is a typical marsh plant, it must be provided with continually wet conditions. Rotted turves and peat are an ideal growing medium, which must never become dry. Feeding is not necessary. Propagate by dividing the clumps. This can be done when repotting.

Pistia stratiotes
Araceae

Water Lettuce (202) is the only member of the genus Pistia. It is found in warm, still water or slow-flowing water courses throughout the tropics. It is most often grown on the surface of pools or aquariums in the home. The leaves, forming a very decorative rosette, are a lovely pale green with prominent venation, mainly on the underside. They are thickly covered with whitish

201

202

Pistia stratiotes—the
inflorescence

hairs. The inflorescence measures 1 cm (⅖ in) and is composed
of several greenish flowers.

It does well indoors if it is provided with sufficiently warm
water — about 20°-25°C (68°-77°F). A flat dish is more suitable
than a tall container for growing this plant. In winter it is best to
remove the plant from the water and put it in sphagnum moss,
which must be kept constantly wet. Propagate by means of the
lateral runners or from seed, the former method being quicker.

PLANTS FOR SUNNY SITUATIONS

Extremely light-loving plants are relatively few in number. They are plants native to open areas where there is no shade of any kind, such as deserts, semi-deserts, steppes, salt marshes and exposed rocks. House plant varieties have, of course, already been adapted by Man. Therefore, cultivated forms of a naturally extremely photophilic species differ in their toleration of the lowered light intensity and shorter overall period of illumination found in the home.

Even the most light-loving plants defend themselves against the harmful effects of direct sunlight by a variety of methods. These include a variously fashioned leaf epidermis, furling the leaf blade, and a covering of hairs. Some plants secrete essential oils that form a kind of protective coat to diffuse the light rays. Besides the intensity and property of light, the duration of daylight is also an important factor. The number of hours of daylight to which a species is adapted depends on the latitude of its natural habitat.

The best places for growing house plants that require lots of light are patios, windowboxes or windowsills facing west, southeast or southwest.

204

205

Plumeria rubra
Apocynaceae

Frangipani (203) is native to Mexico, Venezuela and the Antilles, where it grows as a shrub or small tree with short, rather thick stems marked with numerous scars left by fallen leaves. The branches are thick. Even when it is not in flower, its foliage makes the plant extremely attractive. The leaves are 30-45 cm (12-18 in) long, 15 cm (6 in) wide, leathery and very glossy. During the resting period, which occurs twice a year (in winter and in summer), the leaves fall. The flowers are very fragrant. They are up to 5 cm (2 in) across and, typical of all members of the dogbane family, the petals are spirally furled in the bud. They range in colour from pink to red or purple. Interestingly, one edge of each petal curves inward.

If grown in the home, it must be put in a position in full sunlight and that is also warm; otherwise the plant will not flower. Water only during the growing period.

Passiflora quadrangularis
Passifloraceae

Passion flowers are extremely interesting plants, first and foremost for the structure of their flowers. They are native to the rain forests of Brazil and Peru, where they climb up trees, catching hold with their spirally-coiled tendrils. There are more than 400 species. The generic name is derived from a fancied resemblance of parts of the flower to the instruments of Christ's suffering (Latin *passio* = suffering, *flos* = flower). The specific name of Granadilla (204) refers to the quadrangular glabrous stems. The heart-shaped leaves are 15-20 cm (6-8 in) long; the leaf stalks each have six glands. The fragrant flowers are up to 12 cm (5 in) across with reddish petals and white and violet corona filaments arranged in five rows round the stamens. The large fruits, sometimes more than 20 cm (8 in) in diameter, are edible and are a common food in the tropics. Other species, such as *P. edulis,* also have very tasty fruit. The berries have a very aromatic, slightly sour taste because they contain a lot of

Passiflora edulis
—stem with berry

206

207

citric acid. They are either eaten fresh or used to make soft drinks and to flavour ice cream and other confectionery.

Passion flowers require a high level of humidity and liberal watering in summer. Restrict watering in winter for at least two months; otherwise the plants will not flower. Feed once a week; use a feed with a high concentration of phosphorus and potassium. Propagate from seed, which germinates reliably, or in summer by means of stem or root cuttings. These should be put in a propagator or in a pot filled with compost and covered with a glass jar. They take quite a long time to form roots.

Passiflora caerulea
Passifloraceae

This (205) used to be the most favourite and widely grown of the passion flowers (there are some 400 species). Nowadays, however, when houses are warmer in winter, it is grown less of-

ten because it is impossible to provide the necessary cold and light conditions.

It requires a fairly heavy compost. Position in full sunlight in spring and summer, otherwise it will not flower. The maximum winter temperature is 10°C (50°F). Prune it hard to promote the formation of new, young flower-bearing shoots. Feed weekly from spring to autumn. Propagate either by seed or by cuttings; only ripe stems, with two leaves, should be taken as cuttings. They will readily form roots at a soil temperature of about 20°C (68°F).

Coffea arabica
Rubiaceae

Coffee Tree (206). Even though it is native to the mountains of Ethiopia, it was the Arabs who introduced coffee to the world, hence the specific name. It was first cultivated in the Yemen and only later spread to other countries; it did not reach Amer-

223

ica until the 18th century. It makes a very attractive house plant. The opposite leaves are a glossy dark green and strongly wavy along the secondary veins. This feature makes it easy to identify even when it is not in flower. The fragrant, white flowers are produced throughout the year, so that there may be buds, fully opened flowers as well as fruits on a single plant at the same time. The fruit is a violet-red drupe with two pyrenes, concave on the outer side and flat on the inner side, each containing one seed — the coffee bean.

The Coffee Tree requires a tall pot for it has a long tap root. It should be grown in a mixture of rotted turves, leaf mould and sand. Water liberally and maintain a high level of humidity in summer. Restrict water in winter. It requires quite a high temperature; in winter this should not fall below 15°C (59°F). Propagate by seed, or by air layering in spring or summer.

Rhipsalidopsis rosea
Cactaceae

Easter Cactus (207, 208, 209). All members of the genus Rhipsalidopsis are called 'Easter cacti' because they regularly produce flowers at Easter. They are similar to 'Christmas cacti'. They have rounded, red stem segments, bristly-toothed on the margins. Relatively large, funnel-shaped flowers grow from areoles located at the end of the segments. The fruit is a berry. All these cacti are native to southern Brazil. *R. rosea* (209) is the familiar species. It has vivid pink flowers up to 4 cm (1½ in) across. Another well-known species is *R. gaertneri* (207) with brilliant scarlet red flowers, which grows as an epiphyte in the mountains of Brazil. The hybrid offspring of these two species — *R. × graeseri* (208) — is a very common house plant.

To ensure spring flowering, keep the cactus at a temperature of about 10°C (50°F) for a period of two to three months during the autumn and winter. Then transfer it to a warmer place. Water very sparingly during the resting period, only when the compost is almost dry. The plants grow well even without feeding, but will benefit from an occasional application of a weak solution of compound fertilizer. They do very well in hydroponic containers and are also very attractive in hanging containers or in a dish combined with other plants. Propagate by means of the stem segments.

Pelargonium-Zonale —hybr.
Geraniaceae

the flower

This hybrid (210) is descended chiefly from the South African *P. zonale*. The principal characteristics of this sub-shrub are the upright habit of growth and the rounded, heart-shaped, faintly lobed leaves, softly hairy and with a pronounced darker stripe on the upper side. The inflorescences may have as many as 25 flowers, varying in colour from pink to red, occasionally also white. *P. crispum, P. graveolens, P. capitatum* and *P. tomenosum* have fragrant leaves.

213

Conditions for growing are the same for all Pelargonium species, varieties and cultivars. A suitable growing medium is a mixture of frame soil, leaf mould and compost. Transfer to a cool place in winter, about 10°C (50°F), and restrict watering. Water regularly during the growth period, as drying out even once will cause the leaves to drop. Feed with organic fertilizer. Propagate by means of tip cuttings or side shoots in March or August. Allow them to dry for a few hours before inserting in compost.

**Pelargonium-
Grandiflorum—hybr.**
Geraniaceae

Regal Pelargonium (211) is also a hybrid obtained by many crossings; its parentage includes *P. cucullatum, P. cordatum* and *P. grandiflorum.* The stems turn woody quite soon. The leaves are only faintly lobed, sharply toothed, and when rubbed between the fingers do not give off as strong a scent as those of the preceding species. The flowers are extremely large, about 5 cm (2 in) across, and coloured white, pink, violet or red. The petals have prominent dark patches.

214

215

Pelargonium-	Ivy-leafed Geranium (212) has typical prostrate, faintly angled
Peltatum—hybr.	stems that are usually glabrous. The leaves are long-stalked.
Geraniaceae	usually five-lobed, fleshy and very glossy. They are mostly gla-

Pelargonium-
Peltatum—hybr.
Geraniaceae

Ivy-leafed Geranium (212) has typical prostrate, faintly angled stems that are usually glabrous. The leaves are long-stalked. usually five-lobed, fleshy and very glossy. They are mostly glabrous, but very sparingly hairy on the margin. The flowers may be simple, semi-double or double and variously coloured — for example white, pink, violet or red, depending on the cultivar.

Ardisia crenata
Myrsinaceae

This species (213) is an evergeen shrub or small tree. Its range of distribution extends from Japan to India. The leathery, dark green leaves are very attractive. The pink, 5-merous flowers with joined petals are pretty, and the many small, coral-red berries that remain on the plant for at least six months are an additional decorative feature. The thickened edges of the leaves, inhabited by nitrogen-fixing bacteria living in a symbiotic relationship with the leaf, are typical of the species.

It does well in full sun at normal room temperature. It requires cooler conditions — 15°-18°C (59°-64°F) — in winter. Water regularly. It tends to become leggy, so cut back to within

227

8 cm (3 in) of the base in spring. Propagate by sowing seeds at a temperature of 20°C (68°F). Alternatively, take tip cuttings. These require a temperature of 25°C (77°F) to form roots.

Capsicum frutescens
Solanaceae

Chilli Pepper (214) is widely known primarily as a food plant, but it can also be a very decorative house plant. There are approximately 30 species of Capsicum, all native to America. They were introduced into Europe in the 16th century by the Spaniards. Chilli Pepper is a low-growing shrub about 30 cm (12 in) high, with small, pointed leaves. The flowerhead is circular and coloured white or faintly tinged with yellow. The fruit is globose or pointed and very hot and pungent.

To ensure lots of flowers and fruit that will remain on the plant as attractive ornaments for a long time provide plenty of light and air. The temperature need not be high; a maximum of 20°C (68°F) in summer and 12°-15°C (54°-59°F) in winter. Water liberally. Inadequate watering causes the flowers to drop and the fruits to wither. Feed weekly with compound fertilizer. It is usually grown as an annual. Propagate by sowing seed in February. The seedlings require plenty of light.

217

Punica granatum
Punicaceae

Pomegranate (215) is native to a range from the eastern Mediterranean region to the Himalayas. Its edible fruit has brough about its cultivation throughout the entire sub-tropics. It is often grown in greenhouses as an ornamental plant and can be an unusual and very decorative feature grown in a large container indoors. The cultivar 'Nana' is smaller and hardier. The small glossy leaves and the vermilion red flowers are very attractive. The arrangement of the carpels is unique in the plant kingdom. They are in two whorls, one above the other, so that the ovary has two layers of locules. The fruit, the pomegranate, is a reddish berry with a persistent calyx that contains a large number of seeds with fleshy seed coats. It has a pleasant, acid flavour; the juice is used to flavour the syrup called grenadine. The genus Punica has only two species.

During the growth period, it requires full sun and a humid atmosphere. In winter, it needs lots of light, cool conditions — as low as 0°C (32°F) and limited watering. In summer it may be transferred to the garden. Propagate by tip cuttings and from seed.

Abutilon × hybr.
Malvaceae

Flowering Maple (216) is a hybrid obtained by the crossing of several South American species, chiefly *A. darwinii* and *A. pictum*. It is a long-lived plant with lovely, lobed, maple-like leaves, that may be green or with yellow markings, depending on the cultivar. The flowers also vary in colour and may be yellow, orange or deep red.

The best growing medium is a mixture of heath mould, rotted turves and sand. In summer, the plant requires full sun, but even in winter needs adequate light. If grown in shade, the leaves drop in succession from the bottom up. In summer it may be transferred to a garden, balcony or patio. Water liberally during the growing period. The temperature in winter should be 10°C (50°F). Prune the plant before repotting in early spring. The branches soon make new growth and the shrub is then attractively bushy. The twig cuttings may be used to grow new plants.

218

Aristolochia elegans
—longitudinal section of the flower

219

**Abutilon
megapotamicum**
Malvaceae

This species (217), native to Brazil, has magnificent flowers that open in succession throughout the year. It is a densely-branched shrub, up to 1.5 m (59 in) high, with long, very slender, drooping branches. The leaves are long-stalked. The flowers grow singly from the axils of the leaves on long, thin, pendent stalks. The calyx is inflated and dark purple. The petals are yellow and purple at the base. The anthers are also purple; the filaments are joined to the base, separating only at the top.

A. megapotamicum is more tender than the preceding species. It needs a higher room temperature — up to 25°C (77°F) — but otherwise the requirements for growing it are the same.

Aristolochia elegans
Aristolochiaceae

Calico Plant (218). The flowers, aptly described as 'pipelike' because they are bent like a tobacco pipe, are the most striking feature of all Aristolachias. Those of the Calico Plant, which is native to Mexico, are 10-12 cm (4-4³/₄ in) long with a markedly bent green tube which expands to a broad collar spotted with brownish-purple.

This is a very rewarding and decorative climber that is readily propagated from seed as well as by means of tip cuttings. It often bears flowers in the first year. It requires warm sunlight

231

220

and a humid atmosphere. Aristolochias are also used to cover walls and arbours in the garden; the best species for this purpose is *A. macrophylla.*

Sprekelia
formosissima
Amaryllidaceae

The Jacobean Lily (219) is the only species in the genus Sprekelia; it was formerly assigned to the genus Amaryllis. It is native to Mexico and Guatemala; the bulbs were brought to Europe by the Spanish conquistadors. It has an underground bulb with blood-red stripes. The leaves appear at the same time as or slightly later than the flowers. They are up to 40 cm (16 in) long and only 2 cm (3/4 in) wide. The flowers are borne singly at the end of a long, reddish stem. They are a dark velvety red, measure 8-10 cm (3-4 in) and the petals spread out in a single plane.

It is a semi-desert plant and therefore requires full sun during the growing period. As soon as the plants die back in autumn, lift the bulbs. Clean and store them in a warm, dry place. In March or early April, when the bulbs begin growth, plant them in a nourishing compost with a drainage layer at the bottom of the pot. Propagate by means of the bulb offsets.

Euphorbia pulcherrima
(syn. *Poinsettia*
pulcherrima)
Euphorbiaceae

The Poinsettia (220, 221) is native to Mexico where it may reach a height of 3 m (10 ft). This spurge, the popular Poinsettia, is also called the Christmas Star, for the large red bracts spread out like stars beneath the minute flowers. (The inflorescence is called a cyathium.) Horticulturalists have developed numerous cultivars with different coloured bracts. These may be brilliant

232

or dark red — 'Adventstern von Werder' (220) — white — 'White Wonder', or greenish white — 'White Ecke'. The cultivar 'Plenissima' (221) with a greater number of bracts is very striking. Even when the plant is not in flower its leaves, irregularly lobed and pale green, are a decorative feature.

During the flowering period in winter, it requires full sun and a temperature above 15°C (59°F). Water with tepid water and feed regularly. After the flowers have faded, cut the plant back and give a period of rest in a cool room without watering. Repot and start watering and feeding again in March. Propagate by tip cuttings. Place them in warm water for about one hour after they are taken to check the flow of a milky fluid (lactiferous ducts are a characteristic trait of all spurges). Poinsettia is also used as a cut flower.

Haworthia attenuata
Liliaceae

Almost everyone is familiar with and has probably grown some species of Haworthia. (There are about 160 species, most of which are very decorative plants.) *H. attenuata* (222), like all Haworthias, is native to South Africa. It has been cultivated since the early 19th century. It is a very variable species. The

221

dense rosettes of thick leaves arranged in several rows and often covered with small white tubercles are typical. The upright, simple or branched inflorescences are not particularly attractive, but the leaves are far more decorative. Those of *H. attenuata* are 7 cm (2³/₄ in) long and 15 mm (³/₅ in) wide, sharply pointed, with white, occasionally green, tubercles, arranged in horizontal bands.

It is a fairly easy plant to grow. Normal room temperature is sufficient for good growth, but it will tolerate higher temperatures. Water frequently in summer. Watering the soil is better than spraying, as the leaves tend to rot easily. The more light the plant has, the stiffer the leaves and the whiter the tubercles. Restrict watering in winter. If provided with the proper conditions Haworthias are long-lived plants. They readily produce sideshoots which makes propagation easy.

Aloë variegata
Liliaceae

Many species of Aloë are popular house plants and said to have been cultivated since 1700. Patridge Breast (223) is native to South Africa. The fleshy leaves, crowded in overlapping fashion on a very short stem and usually arranged in three rows, are striking. The white patches on the leaves form irregular horizontal bands. The inflorescence may reach a height of 30 cm (12 in) and is composed of pendent, vermilion flowers with green veins.

222

223

It does well in a light and warm, but well-ventilated place. It is more suitable as an indoor, rather than a greenhouse, plant. Take care when watering to avoid getting water between the leaves, as they may then rot. It makes a great many offsets so that it multiplies at a rapid rate. Even though it often flowers, it rarely produces seeds. The quickest method of propagation is by detaching new plants from the old clump.

Callistemon citrinus
Myrtaceae

This species (224) is the Bottle Brush Plant. The genus Callistemon numbers 25 species native to Australia. The generic name is derived from Greek (*kallos* = beautiful and *stemon* = filament) and truly describes the loveliest organ in the flowers—the stamens with their blood-red filaments. The inflorescence is cylindrical and resembles a brush. The leaves are leathery.

235

224

It does very well indoors, if it is positioned in full sun during the growing period. It requires cooler conditions in winter, with a temperature of 5°-10°C (41°-50°F). Water fairly liberally in summer, but reduce watering in winter. Prune the plant to keep it from becoming too big. It is readily propagated by tip cuttings. They will make roots within several weeks in a mixture of peat and sand at a temperature of about 20°C (68°F).

Stephanotis floribunda The Wax Flower (225) is an evergreen climber with leathery
Asclepiadaceae   leaves resembling those of Hoya; they are 7-9 cm (2³/₄-3¹/₂ in) long, 35-50 mm (1²/₅-2 in) wide and very glossy. Umbels of lovely white blossoms with a pleasant, heady fragrance grow from the axils of the leaves.

To ensure flowering, provide plenty of warmth and light in summer. Mist the plant regularly, particularly in hot summers, and water liberally. It is readily propagated by stem cuttings which should have at least two leaves. They will root within five weeks at a temperature of about 26°C (77°F).

225

Plumbago capensis
(syn. *P. auriculata*)
Plumbaginaceae

This sub-shrub (226) is native to Capetown. The genus Plumbago has only six to ten species found in the tropics and sub-tropics of all continents. It is not commonly grown as a house plant, although it is frequently grown in the greenhouse. The upright to climbing branches are thickly covered with rather small

226

leaves. The terminal inflorescences are composed of profuse blue flowers with tubular, glandular calyx and rotate corolla with extremely narrow corolla tube. The flowers are produced from spring until autumn.

Conditions for growing Wax Flowers are similar to those for growing Pelargoniums. The best growing medium is a clay-peat mixture or rotted turves plus composted soil. It benefits from being moved outdoors in summer so that it has plenty of sun. In winter it requires cool conditions — a temperature of 3°-8°C (37°-46°F) — and plenty of light. It should be pruned hard at the end of winter. The cuttings may be used for propagation; they will root well in a mixture of sand and peat.

Hippeastrum—hybr.
Amaryllidaceae

Hippeastrum (227) is the general designation for this multiple hybrid, commonly called Amaryllis. It is widely grown because its large, bell-like flowers are worth the effort its cultivation requires. A thick stem topped by an umbel of several flowers grows from the large bulb. The leaves are tough and lance-shaped. Since 1800, horticulturists have developed countless

227

228

cultivars through selective breeding and crossing of various species of Hippeastrum. These include ones with flowers coloured red, such as 'Cardinal', pink, such as 'Beautiful Lady', white, such as 'Ludwig's Dazzler', and combinations of these colours.

Hippeastrum must have a period of complete rest, otherwise it will not flower again. Withhold water from mid-August, after which the top parts begin to die back. Store the bulb in a dry place at a temperature of about 10°C (50°F). The new flower stem and leaves begin to grow from the bulb in January. Move it to a warm place and start to water liberally. Feed weekly with a solution of organic fertilizer. It does well in a mixture of two parts leaf mould, and one part each of frame soil, rotted turves and sand. The bulb should be inserted only halfway into the compost so that just the bottom half is covered.

Campanula isophylla
Campanulaceae

Italian Bellflower (228) is the only one of some 300 species in the genus Campanula grown as a pot plant. It is native to Italy. It has thin, trailing stems which are completely concealed by the profusion of flowers in summer. The bell-like corollas open wide and are usually coloured blue, although sometimes they are white; these are typical of the cultivar 'Alba'. The white- and blue-flowered plants are commonly called 'bride' and 'groom'.

The best location for the plant is in a window where it has

239

plenty of light. A suitable compost is a mixture of leaf mould, peat and sand. Water liberally in spring and summer, but because it does not tolerate permanently wet compost, a drainage

231

layer should be put at the bottom of the pot. Feed with compound mineral fertilizer weekly during the growth period. In winter, water sparingly, just so the plants do not dry up. It requires a temperature of 4°-10°C (39°-50°F). As soon as the flowers have faded, prune the plant. Propagate from seed or by tip cuttings.

Petunia—hybr.
Solanaceae

Petunias (229) are native to South America, chiefly to Brazil and Argentina. Shortly after they were introduced into cultivation, they rapidly became the subject of selective breeding. Consequently, there are now countless cultivars with flowers differing not only in colour, but also in size and shape. It is interesting, however, that petunia-lovers tend to prefer forms with simple flowers that are most like the type species.

Petunias are typical window-box, balcony and patio plants. They are annuals, and cultivation ends when the flowers have faded. They are not usually grown from seed by amateurs because it is impossible to provide them with sufficient light. Also, pricking them out is a lengthy task. It is better to buy seedlings from a nursery. Petunias are attractive only in full sun, and they must be watered liberally; otherwise the leaves quickly droop and the flowers wilt.

241

Coleus-Blumei—hybr.
Labiatae

Approximately 150 species of this genus are distributed throughout the tropics. *Coleus blumei* (230) is the principal parent species of numerous hybrids, which mainly differ in the colour of the leaves. The extraordinary colour combinations can probably be matched only by the Crotons.

The more sun the plants have, the more intense the colours. Coleus may be grown from seed but a more rapid method of propagation is by cuttings. It is best to take these from non-flowering plants. Older specimens are not attractive, so it is best to grow new plants each year.

Begonia-
Tuberhybrida—hybr.
Begoniaceae

tuber commencing growth

Begonias (231) are frequently grown in windowboxes or in pots on the windowsill. They flower from spring until autumn. A profusion of large flowers of various colours — white, pink, red or yellow — is the reward for the relatively little care the plants require.

Before the first frost, cut off the top parts of the plant just above the tuber. Store the tubers in peat in a dark room or cellar, where the temperature does not drop below freezing point. In February, transfer the tubers into sand so they will put out

232

233

roots. Plant them in compost and transfer to a windowbox in late May. Water liberally and feed once a week with a solution of compound or organic fertilizer. Propagate by cutting old tubers into pieces—each piece must have an eye.

Mimosa pudica
Leguminosae

Sensitive Plant (232) is native to the tropical regions of Brazil where it eventually becomes woody. Few plants react to being touched as quickly as the Sensitive Plant. The moment a stalk or leaflet is touched, the plant responds immediately by folding the leaflets and drooping the leaves. This movement is distinct and noticeable. It can take as long as 30 minutes before the leaves return to their normal position. The minute, pinkish-violet flowers are clustered in globose heads.

It is often grown for one year and then a new plant is raised from seed. The seeds germinate readily and, under the right conditions, the growth of the young plants is rapid. It requires

abundant warmth, water and sun. It is sensitive to soil temperature, which should not fall below 18°C (64°F) during the growing period. It must never become too dry and must not be grown in shade. If it is overwintered at a temperature of 12°-15°C (54°-59°F) the Sensitive Plant may be cultivated for a number of years.

Feijoa sellowiana
(syn. *Acca sellowiana*)
Myrtaceae

This species (233) is native to Brazil and Uruguay. It has been cultivated since 1815. It is a pity that it is not commonly grown in the home. It is more usually cultivated in the greenhouse, although it is an undemanding plant. It is an evergreen shrub or, less often, a small tree with silvery twigs and buds. The leaves are opposite, elliptic to ovate, 3-8 cm (1-3 in) long and 2-4 cm (³/₄-1¹/₂ in) wide. They are dark green on the upper surface and white on the underside. The silvery colouring is very attractive, but the flowers are the most decorative feature. These grow singly from the axils of the leaves and measure about 4 cm

(1½ in) across. The four, spoon-like petals are white with a red centre. The stamens, which may be up to 25 mm (⁹⁄₁₀ in) long, have carmine-red filaments and yellow anthers. The fruit is a yellow-green, ovoid berry, 5 cm (2 in) long with remnants of the calyx at the tip. It has a pleasant, pear-like taste.

It requires plenty of light and a high temperature in summer and cool conditions in winter. Propagation is difficult because cuttings do not root very easily.

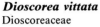

Dioscorea vittata
Dioscoreaceae

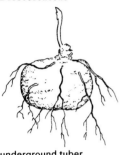

underground tuber
commencing growth

Although it is not demanding, this plant (234) is rarely encountered in the home. It is grown not for its flowers, but for its ornamental foliage. However, it has one disadvantage; the leaves drop and the plant dies back in the autumn. Once the rest period is over, its growth is extremely vigorous and it again attains a fine size. The variegated leaves are patterned on the upper side with silvery, arching veins and silvery patches in the middle; they are carmine-red on the underside.

Store the underground tubers at a temperature of 15°-18°C (59°-64°F) in winter. In late March, plant them in nourishing compost and start watering with care until they become rooted. Water fairly liberally and mist the leaves regularly during the growing season.

235

Gardenia jasminoides
Rubiaceae

Gardenia (235), native to China, was named after the 18th-century naturalist Alexander Garden. It is a shrub reaching a height of more than 1.5 m (59 in) with opposite, leathery leaves and large stipules. The striking, pure white, sweetly scented blooms grow at the ends of the branches and are sessile. There is a wide range of cultivars: 'Plena' with double flowers, 'Veitchiana' with double flowers timed to bloom at Christmas and 'Fortuniana' with extraordinarily large flowers resembling camellia blossoms, for example.

It requires a sunny position. Water liberally and mist regularly, but not during the flowering period. Always use soft water and a lime-free compost. Gardenia is sensitive to temperature fluctuations. Propagate by tip cuttings that will make roots within three weeks in sandy compost at a soil temperature of about 20°-25°C (68°-77°F). After they are rooted, the plants should be pruned to promote bushy growth. Gardenia is also used for cut flowers.

Crinum × powellii
Amaryllidaceae

There are more than 100 species of Crinum distributed throughout the tropics and sub-tropics, mostly in coastal regions. Powell's Swamp Lily (236) grows from a large, long-necked, globose bulb. The strap-shaped leaves may be up to 1 m (39 in) long and have an entire margin. The flowers are generally borne in clusters of eight at the end of a long stem. They are funnel-like, tinted pink, and their stalks are 4 cm (1½ in) long. There are many cultivars with white, pink or red flowers.

It does best in cooler conditions, so it is important to put it in a room that is not too warm. It should be placed by a window with direct sunlight. Water liberally, but the compost should not become soggy. Limit watering in winter, when the plant should be kept at a maximum temperature of 8°C (46°F). Propagate by bulb offsets.

Zantedeschia
aethiopica
Araceae

The Calla Lily (237) was a traditional flower of bridal bouquets, but it is also often grown as a house plant. Like Sansevieria, it is almost indestructible. It is native to South Africa, where it grows in muddy meadows that dry out in summer. It has magnificent blooms with white, cornucopia-like spathes and yellow, narrowly cylindrical spadices.

237

PLANTS FOR SHADED SITUATIONS

Some ornamental plants require shade or will do well or will tolerate a shaded or partially shaded location. They are mostly plants of the tropical rain forests. These forests have a huge tree layer, which is usually differentiated into three height levels. At the uppermost level are single trees, 50-60 m (160-200 ft) high. They have broad crowns which even though they do not form a closed canopy, reduce the intensity of the sunlight. The trees of the crowded middle level, 25-40 m (80-130 ft) high, have narrower crowns. The lower level of shrubs and trees, 10-15 m (30-50 ft) high, is composed of species that, at the very least, like partial shade. Furthermore, they are often covered with lianas trying to get at least a little more light. The herbaceous layer consists almost entirely of perennial species. The herbaceous layer has the smallest number of different species.

When growing house plants native to the tropical rain forest, bear in mind that they are mostly plants that grow in permanent shade and, if they do grow in light, then they do not tolerate direct sunlight. Larger glassed enclosures, such as a greenhouse or conservatory, should be shaded in summer with screens or by coating the glass with white or blue paint. Plants placed close by a window can be shaded quite simply by curtains or shutters. Otherwise, they can be moved farther away from the window for the duration of summer.

The effect of light on plants is not restricted to its duration and intensity. In a shaded location, the temperature on a plant's surface is lower than that on a plant growing in the sun. The slower rate of evaporation in plants growing in partially shaded or shaded locations also plays a role. The tissues of such plants are far less adapted to the loss of water and to fluctuations between daytime and night-time temperatures.

240

Anthurium-Scherzerianum—hybr.
(syn. *A.* × *hortulanum*)
Araceae

Anthuriums (238) are very decorative plants grown not only for their blooms, but also gor their foliage. In European conditions they are typical greenhouse plants, but are also quite frequently grown in modern, centrally-heated houses. However, it can be difficult to provide them with a sufficiently humid atmosphere.

241

The original type species, *A. scherzerianum*, native to Costa Rica and Guatemala, is not grown as a house plant; only the cultivars obtained by crossing this species with other species of Anthurium are grown in the home. The spathe (enlarged ornamental bract) of hybrids is vivid red, white, green, yellow or even dark red. Occasionally it may be blotched. The inflorescence is called a spadix. It consists of a thickened axis covered with numerous small flowers. Because the blooms are so extraordinarily beautiful and long-lived they are also very popular as cut flowers.

All species of Anthurium should be grown in diffused light. They are thermophilous plants, so do not allow the temperature to fall below 18°C (64°F) in winter. To ensure sufficient moisture and humidity, wrap the pot in damp moss or put it in a larger container and fill the space in between with moss. Anthuriums require a nourishing, free-draining compost, such as a mixture of peat, heath mould, sand and charcoal. Cover the surface with moist moss. A loam and peat substrate is also good. Anthuriums also do well in hydroponic containers. The most rapid method of propagation is by dividing older plants.

Anthurium-Andreanum—hybr.
(syn. *A. cultorum*)
Araceae

This (239) is a very familiar plant for, like the preceding species, it is grown for cutting and is widely sold by florists. The cut flowers may last several weeks in a vase. The red spathe and slender, twisted, yellow spadix make an attractive contrast. It is

251

becoming increasingly popular as a pot plant. The conditions for growing it indoors are the same as for the species described above.

Anthurium pedatoradiatum
Araceae

This species (240) from Mexico has leaves with finger-like lobes, whereas most anthuriums have leaves with entire margins. It is usually grown in a greenhouse or conservatory, rather than in a living room because it is so big.

Aglaonema crispum
(syn. *A. roebelinii*)
Araceae

The genus Aglaonema includes about 50 species distributed throughout tropical Asia, where they are usually found in the undergrowth of forests. *A. crispum* (241) is admired for the lovely markings on its leaves. Indeed, it was the foliage that aroused interest in growing this tropical, Malaysian species as a house plant. It is a perennial, reaching a height of about 1 m (39 in). The stems are thickly covered with short-stalked leaves. The tough, leathery leaf blades, 20-30 cm (8-12 in) long and 8-13 cm (3-5 in) wide are beautifully patterned in dark green and silvery grey. The inflorescences are relatively long, greenish and inconspicuous. They attract greater attention when they have developed into red berries. These remain on the plant for a long time.

It requires warm conditions throughout the year and diffused

243

244

light or partial shade; it does not tolerate direct sunlight. Water liberally so that the root ball is permanently moist but not muddy. The compost should be nourishing and free-draining; a mixture of leaf mould, peat and sand is suitable. Bowls are preferable to taller containers. The plant can easily be propagated by dividing clumps or by stem cuttings. It can also be propagated by seed which germinates reliably.

Aglaonema commutatum
(syn. *A. treubii*)
Araceae

Ribbon Aglaonema (242) may reach a height of 1 m (39 in) but, because the leaves on the lower part of the stem drop leaving only a cluster at the top, specimens that grow too tall are usually unattractive. They should, therefore, be cut back and the old stems left in the pot. They soon make new growth (this applies to other species as well). The cuttings should be put either in

253

water or moist compost to root. This species is readily identified by the narrower leaves which are up to 30 cm (12 in) long, with ash-grey markings on the upper side. Conditions for growing are the same as for *A. crispum* (see p. 252).

Aglaonema costatum
Araceae

This species (243) is native to southwestern Malaysia. It has a very short stem with crowded leaves. The leaf blade is pointed ovate, about 12-22 cm (4³/₄-8¹/₂ in) long, and 7-12 cm (2³/₄-4³/₄ in) wide. The leaves are dark green with a white midrib and blotches. The flowers are tiny and arranged in a spadix — the typical inflorescence of aroids — enclosed by a whitish-green

245

254

spathe. The one-seeded ovoid bright red berries are more spectacular than the flowers. They may remain on the plant for several months.

Its indoor cultivation is very easy, but it must be provided with a high level of humidity. It is a long-lived plant. As soon as it begins to grow too tall, it should be cut back. Put cuttings in water and plant in compost after they have produced roots. Put several cuttings in one pot so the new plants will make a richer display.

247

Aglaonema pictum
Araceae

This Aglaonema (244) is native to Sumatra and Borneo. It has been cultivated since 1880. The lower part of the stem is branched and prostrate. The leaf stalks are 3-5 cm (1-2 in) long, the leaf blades 10-20 cm (4-8 in) long and 4-5 cm (1$\frac{1}{2}$-2 in) wide. The irregular white blotches stand out in sharp contrast to the deep green of the leaves.

As a house plant, it is not only hardy but also extremely decorative. It has no special light requirements and so can be grown quite far from a window. Cultivation and propagation are the same as for the preceding species of Aglaonema.

248

**Dieffenbachia picta
'Bausei'**
Araceae

Dieffenbachias (245) are native to tropical America, where some 30 species grow. They were introduced into Europe in the mid-19th century; to England and Belgium first, and then their cultivation rapidly spread to other countries. They are named in honour of J. Dieffenbach (1796-1863), head gardener of the Botanical Gardens in Vienna. They are distributed from Mexico and the Antilles to Peru. Many species readily interbreed. All have stout upright stems that become woody and are thickly covered with long, sheath-like stalks that embrace the stem. The leaf blades are usually ovate with a prominent midrib and are decoratively patterned with blotches, marbling or stripes. They are greatly prized as houseplants for their ornamental foliage.

257

The inflorescence is not very conspicuous — a spadix with a relatively narrow spathe. *D. picta* has large leaves with stalks about 10-20 cm (4-8 in) long and blades 15-30 cm (6-12 in) long and 10-15 cm (4-6 in) wide. They are usually yellow-green, with relatively few, dark green blotches that merge to form a dark band on the margin. The yellow often fades to white.

It is not difficult to grow. It requires warm conditions, and can be grown equally well in a heated greenhouse and indoors at normal room temperature. It does not tolerate direct sunlight, preferring partial shade. However, it does need adequate light for healthy growth and colourful leaves. It does not have a distinct period of rest but watering should be limited during the cooler months from November to February. It requires a minimum winter temperature of 16°C (60°F). In summer, water liberally and do not allow the compost to become too dry. Feed weekly during the growing period. Like all Dieffenbachias, this one is readily propagated by stem or tip cuttings which may be taken at any time of the year. Because they are poisonous and can cause painful, ugly swellings on the hands, the plants must be cut back with great care.

250

Dieffenbachia maculata
(syn. *D. picta*)
Araceae

This species (246), from Brazil, is one of the most widely grown. Its stout stem can reach a height of more than 1 m (39 in). The leaf blades, broadly elliptic with a heart-shaped base and a pointed tip, are patterned with irregular white blotches. The spathe and spadix are greenish. It is extremely variable and includes several geographic varieties. Moreover, horticulturists have developed numerous cultivars that are difficult to distinguish from one another, and that often resemble cultivated varieties of the closely related species *D. seguina*. Probably the most familiar cultivar of *D. maculata* is 'Julius Roehrs'; the juvenile form has yellow-green leaves and only the midribs and margins are coloured green. It was developed in the USA in 1936 and its large-scale cultivation started some 11 years later.

Dieffenbachia amoena
Araceae

This (247, 248) has large, obovate leaves coloured dark green with yellowish or cream-white blotches, rather like stripes between the secondary veins. The cultivar 'Mariana' (248) differs from the type by having leaves with large, pale patches that are white rather than yellowish. Quite often, even the midrib is not green but a pale colour. Growing requirements are the same as for other Dieffenbachias.

Peperomia caperata
Piperaceae

Peperomias (249) are herbs that often have fleshy to leathery leaves and a developed or suppressed stem. Formerly the genus was said to include approximately 600 species but nowadays, with the trend to divide large species into smaller ones, it is estimated that there are some 1,000 distributed in Asia, Africa, Central and South America. Although they are ideal plants for room decoration, the assortment grown as house plants is not as wide as the genus merits. It could be said that almost all Peperomias are suitable for growing indoors. *P. caperata* greatly resembles

252

the widely cultivated species, *P. hederaefolia* (syn. *P. griseo-argentea* hort.). It forms thick clumps of long-stalked leaves; the stalks, tinged faintly pink, are juicy and at the same time stiff; the relatively small blade is 6 cm (2¹/₂ in) long, ovate with a heart-shaped base and greatly wrinkled along the veins. It is coloured fresh green, changing to olive-green by the veins and even to chocolate-brown towards the stalk. The underside of the leaf is pale green. The leaves of *P. hederaefolia* are silver and glossy on the upper surface, and greenish-white on the underside. The distinctive feature of *P. caperata* is its regularity in flowering. However, the upright narrow inflorescences are not very striking. Those who want to grow Peperomias for their flowers should choose *P. fraseri* with white, fragrant blooms.

A suitable compost is a mixture of leaf mould, frame soil, peat and sand, or a loam and peat substrate, with a pH of about 6. Because it is found chiefly in the undergrowth of trop-

Peperomia—rooted leaf
and tip cutting

253

ical rain forests where it is accustomed to dim light and dampness, it does well indoors in a humid atmosphere, in a kitchen or bathroom, for example. Regular misting also supplies humidity. It will not tolerate direct sunlight; the leaves turn an unattractive yellow. It grows well in hydroponic containers and is extremely decorative in mixed plant arrangements. Propagate by stem cuttings or with leaves (a method that is not very common). Insert them in very sandy compost and, as soon as they make roots, plant them, two or three to a pot. The most suitable time is spring or autumn.

Peperomia obtusifolia
Piperaceae

This Peperomia (250, 251), like most others, is native to tropical America. It has an upright or ascending, completely glabrous stem. The leaves are opposite, elliptic to obovate, and 5-12 cm (2-4³/₄ in) long, 3-5 cm (1-2 in) wide. Unlike those of its closest relative *P. clusiifolia*, they are distinctly stalked. The type has uniformly green leaves, while those of the cultivar 'Variegata'

(250) have typical yellow-white markings. The cultivar 'Velli' (251) has tricoloured leaves. The flowers, arranged in upright spikes, are small and inconspicuous; each has only two stamens and one style.

It can either be grown by itself or in a pot or a bowl with other plants. It may even be grown as an epiphyte; in which case insert the roots in light compost for epiphytes, wrapped in a ball of moss to retain moisture.

Aeschynanthus speciosus
Gesneriaceae

This species (252) is native to Java, Borneo and Malaysia. It is an epiphyte, grown not only for its lovely, large flowers, but also for its foliage. The leaves are opposite, sometimes in groups of three, leathery and glossy on the upper side, and faintly crenate on the margins. The flowers, almost 10 cm (4 in) long, are borne in terminal clusters of 6-12 flowers at the ends of long shoots measuring up to 1 m (39 in). The green calyces are only 8 mm ($^3/_{10}$ in) long, but the corollas are striking. They

254

are completely covered with fine hairs and the tube is coloured yellow-orange with a scarlet-red mouth. The stamens and the pistil protrude prominently from the tube. It is a very decorative subject for hanging containers.

It requires adequate light but, like most plants of the tropical rain forests, it does not tolerate direct sunlight. The best growing medium is a mixture of equal parts of peat, frame soil and sand, wrapped in a ball of sphagnum moss to retain moisture. Maintain a temperature of 22°-25°C (72°-77°F). Water regularly and do not allow the compost to dry out. Mist in dry conditions.

Peperomia argyreia
(syn. *P. arifolia*
var. *argyreia*)
Piperaceae

This species (253), native to Brazil, unlike other Peperomias, has shield-like leaves which serve as a ready means of identification. The stem is greatly abbreviated, so the long-stalked leaves grow in the form of a rosette. The red leaf stalks are striking. The leaf blade is broadly ovate, 8-12 cm (3-4³/₄ in) long, glabrous on both sides and with broad white bands between the veins on the upper surface. Shield-like leaves, that is, ones where the stalk emerges from the centre of the blade, are quite unusual; other familiar examples are the leaves of the tropical lotus *Nelumbo nucifera*, and of the nasturtium *Tropaeolum majus*, commonly grown in the garden and in the windowbox.

Conditions for successful growth are the same as for the pre-

256

ceding Peperomias. It is readily propagated by means of the leaves.

Saxifraga stolonifera 'Tricolor'
Saxifragaceae

Aaron's Beard or Mother-of-Thousands (254) is a good choice plant for cooler rooms. It is native to the mountains of China and Japan. It makes a good rosette of round, crinkly-edged, long-stalked leaves; those of the cultivar 'Tricolor' are creamy yellow to pink on the margin. The small white flowers are arranged in tall, racemose inflorescences. The two, enlarged, all-white petals are striking; the other three are smaller with pale violet tips. Long, thread-like runners, bearing baby plants at the end, emerge from the leaf rosette.

The trailing runners make this Saxifraga an ideal plant for positioning on a high shelf or in a hanging container. The best growing medium is frame or composted soil with an addition of coarse sand. The type species tolerates a temperature as low as 5°C (41°F) in winter, but the cultivar 'Tricolor' is more tender and grows best at a temperature of 15°-20°C (59°-68°F). Water moderately, but mist regularly to provide a very humid atmosphere. Feed with organic fertilizer.

Begonia-Elatior —hybr.
Begoniaceae

This (255) is one of many Begonias grown for their ornamental flowers. It is a hybrid developed in England by crossing *B. soco-trana* and the cultivar *B. tuberhybrida* 'Viscountess'. The rich

265

257

clusters of pink to red, often double flowers are very attractive. The dense, compact and glossy foliage is also decorative. Although this is a hybrid offspring of a tuberous Begonia, it does not form tubers.

Cultivation is not difficult. It requires a light position, sheltered from direct sunlight. Use a compost with plenty of peat. It requires a temperature of 20°-22°C (68°-72°F) in the growing season; in winter do not allow the temperature to fall below 18°C (64°F). Water liberally and feed at one to two week intervals during the growing period. It is readily propagated by stem cuttings taken from April to May.

Begonia ×
tuberhybrida
'Pendula'
Begoniaceae

This (256) tuberous-rooted trailing Begonia was obtained by crossing tuberous Begonias with certain small-flowered species or cultivars. It is very well suited for growing in hanging containers or a windowbox. The trailing stems bear relatively small leaves and numerous medium-sized flowers.

In February, put tubers that have been overwintered into sandy compost so that they are covered about three-quarters of the way up; keep the compost moist. They will soon make new growth and, when the plants are about 8-10 cm (3-4 in) high, transfer them to pots or windowboxes. They may be repotted a second time, if desired. If they are to be grown on the windowsill, do not put them outside until late May. A suitable growing medium is a mixture of two parts leaf mould and one part each of peat, compost, pine-leaf mould and sand. An ideal position is one in partial shade that is not exposed to a draught when the room is aired. In late September, lift the tubers and cut off the green top parts. Let the tubers dry. Remove any remaining compost and store them in peat in a dry, frost-free place for the winter.

Begonia masoniana
Begoniaceae

The Iron Cross Begonia (257) was introduced into Europe from China in 1959. Its common name is derived from the shape of the markings on the leaves. It is one of the loveliest Begonias, grown not for its flowers, but for its ornamental foliage. It is a robust plant with a large tuber, reddish stems covered with white hairs, and large pointed leaves about as long as they are wide. The leaf blades look very attractive, coloured green with contrasting dark markings. They are very wrinkled and covered with numerous red hairs.

It does best in places where it gets light from two sides. Direct

258

sunlight damages the leaves, and too much shade causes them to become unattractively long and poorly coloured. It grows well in a loam and peat substrate, and cannot tolerate either very wet or very dry conditions. It requires fairly high temperatures; in winter, it should not fall below 20°C (68°F). Young plants require an even higher temperature. Feed every week or two weeks during the growing season, but only very occasionally in winter. Propagation of all foliage Begonias is simple. Because they have strong powers of regeneration, they can be propagated by leaf cuttings, by the rootstock or by stem cuttings. These make roots best in peat at a soil temperature of 25°C (77°F) and in a very humid atmosphere.

Begonia-Rex—hybr.
Begoniaceae

It is astonishing how variable the genus Begonia is and how many species it includes. It is estimated that there are some 1,000 species and as many as 10,000 cultivars. Despite their great diversity, they all have the same flower structure and asymmetrical leaves. *Begonia rex* (258) has beautiful leaves and this makes it a popular house plant. They are long-stalked, roughly triangular with pointed tips and faintly heart-shaped bases. They may be up to 30 cm (12 in) long, 12-20 cm (5-8 in) wide, and wavy and long-bristled on the margins. Their gorgeous colour is very striking. They are not green, but carmine-red with shades of brown to black, often with patches of silver.

This Begonia is often subject to attack by fungi, particularly in houses where it does not have enough warmth and is overwatered. Not only is the white coating on the leaves unattractive, but also the fungi cause the plant's roots to die. Propagation is very easy by means of leaf cuttings which rapidly root in contact with the compost.

Saintpaulia ionatha
Gesneriaceae

flowers of various cultivars

African Violet (259, 260) has, in fact, nothing in common with violets; it is not even related, for it belongs to a family very distant from the Violaceae family. Perhaps only the similar blue-violet colour of the blooms gave rise to its popular name. It is native to Africa, the home of the 20 other species of the genus. It grows from sea level to a height of 2,000 m (6,600 ft) usually in the undergrowth of rain forests. Horticulturists have developed a great many cultivars that differ chiefly in the colour of the flowers. These may be white, pink, blue or blue-violet, such as the cultivars 'Alba', 'Rosakönigin' and 'Blaukönigin'. Others may have crinkly-edged petals such as 'Mayfair', and still others have leaves with crinkled margins, for example 'Crispa'.

Once you have grown an African Violet, you will surely want to continue, because it is a fairly undemanding plant that is readily propagated and produces flowers almost without stopping. It should be grown in a small pot. To maintain the dark green colour of the leaves, shade it from direct sun. Exposure to direct sun results in unattractive, pale leaves. A mixture of leaf mould, peat and sand is a suitable growing medium. It will produce flowers almost the whole year at a temperature of about 20°C (68°F). A temperature of 25°C (68°F) in summer will promote even more profuse flowering. Take care when watering

260

261

not to splash the leaves for then they become spotted and soon rot. Propagate by means of the leaves. Put the leaf stalks in water to root or insert them directly into sand or compost. New plants can also be grown from the leaf blade.

**Rhoeo spathacea
'Variegata'**
(syn. *R. discolor*)
Commelinaceae

The Boat Lily (261) is the only species in the genus Rhoeo. It has spread from Central America throughout practically all tropical regions. It often grows as an epiphyte. It resembles Tradescantia to which it is related; both belong to the same family. However, it is not suitable for hanging containers and is grown only in pots. The ornamental leaves are stiff, up to 35 cm (14 in) long and 35-70 mm ($1^2/5$-$2^3/4$ in) wide. They grow upwards at a slant and are coloured a striking dark violet on the underside. The white, 3-merous flowers grow from the axils of the leaves between two spoon-like bracts. Both the type and the popular cultivar 'Variegata' (261) with yellow-striped leaves are grown indoors. If placed in a light position the leaves are attractively variegated, but the plant does not tolerate direct sunlight.

Normal room temperature is sufficient; in winter the temperature should not fall below 16°C (61°F). The growing medium should contain peat. Water and mist the plant regularly to maintain a relative humidity of about 50-60 per cent. Propagate by means of sideshoots.

Asparagus plumosus
(syn. *A. setaceus*)
Liliaceae

Several species of Asparagus are popular houseplants and the cut fronds are often used for bouquets, as well as for flower arrangements. There are nearly 300 species in the genus, distributed throughout the Old World. The two most widely encountered are *A. plumosus* (262) and *A. densiflorus*. The minute leaves are typical. They are often only scale-like or spine-like and their function of photosynthesis is taken over by the flattened branches resembling needle-like or linear leaves. These are

262

called phylloclades or cladophylls. The 3-merous flowers indicate that the plant belongs to the lily family. The fruit is a berry. The greatly branched stems with numerous phylloclades are typical of *A. plumosus*. These are needle-like spines, 3-5 mm (¹/₁₀-¹/₅ in) long and growing in clusters of 6-12. The leaves are spine-like and faintly curved. The minute flowers, opening in the autumn, grow singly on very short flower stems that are 1 mm (¹/₂₀ in) long.

It is quite a demanding plant. It requires plenty of light and a high winter temperature. In summer, it also requires a high level of humidity so frequent and regular misting is essential. Repot every year. At the same time, the plant may be divided to obtain new specimens.

Asparagus densiflorus
'Meyeri'
(syn. *A. sprengeri*)
Liliaceae

This Asparagus (263), native to Africa (Natal), has a great many arching stems that are woody at the base. The spine-like leaves are only 3 mm (¹/₁₀ in) long and faintly curved. The phylloclades are usually in pairs, 15-30 cm (6-12 in) long, 1-2 mm (¹/₂₀-¹/₁₀ in) wide, and pointed. The fragrant flowers are white and extremely small. The ripe berries are red. The cultivar 'Meyeri', currently becoming very popular with horticulturists, was developed from this species. Its branches crowded with numerous phylloclades makes it look like a bushy fox tail. They may be up to 1 m (39 in) long and look very attractive.

Apart from *A. plumosus*, Asparagus species grown indoors usually require a relatively low temperature — normal room temperature in summer, 10°-15°C (50°-59°F) in winter. Water frequently. Propagate by dividing old clumps (the underground roots are thickened like tubers) or by seed. Pick the berries in **264**

February, remove the seeds, put them in peaty compost and cover them with dark plastic foil so no light penetrates; the seeds will germinate only in darkness. The best temperature for germination is 22°C (72°F).

Cyperus alternifolius
Cyperaceae

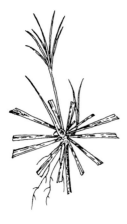

Cyperus—vegetative propagation from buds on the leaves

Plants of the genus Cyperus are not only very ornamental but have a long history of being useful to Man. There is no need to point out how useful the species *C. papyrus* was from about 3000 B.C. when the Egyptians began to make a writing material from its pith. *C. esculentus*, with its edible tubers, was also important. *C. alternifolius*, or Umbrella Plant (264), is native to Madagascar and the neighbouring islands, where it often forms impenetrable growths on the shores of lakes and water courses. It has now become a common household plant. In cultivation it reaches a height of 50-100 cm (20-39 in) and forms dense clumps. The leaves, 25 cm (9 in) long and 1 cm (²/₅ in) wide, grow at the ends of triangular stems, a typical characteristic of the Cyperaceae family.

It is very well suited to growing in a paludarium. If it is grown in a pot, this must be placed in a dish of water. The Umbrella Plant withstands high temperatures — as high as 30°C (86°F) in summer — but also grows well at normal room temperatures. A popular growing medium is a mixture of frame soil, compost and sand. It requires a light position for good growth. Propagate by dividing clumps. Alternatively, if you want to keep thick clumps, cut off a rosette of leaves with a stem 1 cm (²/₅ in) long and put it in water to root. Cutting off part of the leaf blades to shorten them by as much as two thirds is recommended.

Cyperus diffusus
Cyperaceae

This species (265) is about 90 cm (35 in) high with basal leaves almost the same length but only 5-15 mm ($^1/_5$-$^1/_2$ in) wide and rough-margined. The leaves at the end of each stem, numbering 6-12, are up to 30 cm (12 in) long and about 1 cm ($^2/_5$ in) wide.

It grows best in a greenhouse, but it also does well as a house plant in a container with wet compost standing in a dish constantly filled with water. It may also be cultivated in an aquarium or paludarium. A nourishing compost is essential. It is readily propagated by tip cuttings, like *C. alternifolius* (see above). Put them in water or wet sand. Then plant in pots as soon as they form roots. Propagation from seed is a very lengthy and time-consuming job.

Euonymus japonicus
Celastraceae

This evergreen shrub (266) is the only species of Euonymus, comprising nearly 170 species, that is cultivated as a house plant. Most popular are the small-leaved cultivars. Some, like

266

'Microphyllus' and 'Microphyllus Aureo-Variegatus' have yellow markings. In its native habitat in Japan and Korea, it reaches a height of 5-8 m (16-26 ft). The glossy, dark green leaves are obovate to elongate, crenate, and 3-7 cm (1-2³/₄ in) long. It bears flowers only relatively rarely indoors. The flowers are small and white; the fruits are light red. It is often used for decoration in entrance halls, corridors, exhibition rooms and concert halls. In warmer regions, it may be grown outdoors in a sheltered position.

It requires light, but not direct sunlight, and good ventilation. In summer it is best to transfer it outdoors to a partially shaded position. Water frequently so that it does not dry out. In winter the plant should be kept in a cool room at a temperature of 5°-10°C (41°-50°F). Propagate by tip cuttings. Insert them in a mixture of peat and sand at a temperature of about 18°C (64°F). As soon as the plants are well rooted, they must be pruned to promote bushy growth.

Rhododendron-Simsii —hybr.
Ericaceae

Indian Azalea (267, 268) is a hybrid derived from *R. simsii*, a species found in China and Taiwan. The first azaleas brought to Europe in 1808 were already hybrids from some Japanese garden. Because they caught the fancy of horticulturists, they soon became the object of extensive cross-breeding, chiefly in

Belgium and Germany. As a result, there are now vast numbers of cultivars, categorized according to their flowering period into three groups: early, semi-early, and late flowering. Each group includes many cultivars that differ in the form or colour of the flowers (semi-double, double, pink, violet, etc.).

The Indian Azalea requires diffused light. It is usually transferred to a partially shaded location in the garden from May to September. When it is moved back indoors, maintain a temperature at 5°-12°C (41°-54°F). As soon as the buds begin to swell, raise the temperature to 18°C (64°F). It is best grown in a mixture of peat, heath or pine-leaf mould and sand. It is a lime-hating plant. The compost must be coarse and porous with a pH of about 4. Water liberally in summer, even twice a day if necessary. In winter, when the plant is not in flower, water sparingly, but do not allow it to dry out. Rainwater is best; in any case, do not use water that contains lime. After the flowers have fin-

269

270

ished, the plant must be moved to a larger container. Even though azaleas are used for room decoration only until they finish flowering, if cared for properly, they will last a number of years.

Clivia miniata
Amaryllidaceae

Kafir Lily (269) is a popular house plant. Besides having beautiful flowers and attractive foliage, it is very easy to care for. It was brought from its natural habitat in South Africa to England in 1854 and rapidly became widely grown for room decoration. It does not grow from a bulb like plants of the related genus Hippeastrum, but has pale fleshy roots. The closely sheathed leaves taper upwards to a height of 40-60 cm (16-24 in); they are 4-6 cm (1½-2½ in) wide. The orange-red flowers with yellow throats are borne in umbels at the end of a stout, flattened stem. The berries are green for a long time, later turning bright red.

The flowers appear in spring, but if the plant is given proper care, it may produce a second crop in the autumn.

When the plant begins to form flowers, water it with tepid water. As soon as the flowers have faded, cut them off to prevent the plant's expending unnecessary energy on the formation of seeds. Sometimes it does not produce flowers. This is usually because it did not have a rest period in winter. Transfer it to a cool place (at a temperature of 10°-15°C (50°-59°F) in winter. Withhold water almost entirely for about two months. It is rapidly propagated by means of sideshoots.

Primula malacoides
Primulaceae

Fairy Primrose (270) is one of about 500 species of Primula. It is native to China, where it grows at elevations of 2,000-3,000 m (6,600-9,900 ft), but may often be found at lower elevations, in rice fields, for example, where it occurs as a weed. Primulas are not only popular plants for growing in the garden, but also for growing indoors. *P. obconica, P. sinensis* (syn. *P. praenitens*) and

P. malacoides are particularly popular as house plants. The leaves of *P. malacoides* are longish-ovate, faintly lobed and fresh green in colour. The delicate flowers appear as early as February. They grow in whorls of two to five above each other. They may be simple, semi-double or double and may range in colour from white through pink and red to violet.

To produce blooms over a long period, it requires plenty of light but it rapidly wilts if exposed to direct sunlight. Water liberally but take care not to overwater. Because it is an annual it need not be repotted or fed. Propagate by seed. This may be difficult in the beginning because the seeds are extremely small and the germinating seedlings are minute.

Piper nigrum
Piperaceae

Black Pepper (271) is known chiefly as a food plant; its berries are the most widely consumed of all seasonings (black and white pepper). It is also a rewarding and, above all, undemanding ornamental climbing plant. It is native to tropical Asia

where it reaches a height of 10 m (33 ft). The leaves are alternate, heart-shaped and dark green. The green flowers are extremely small and arranged in drooping clusters. They do not have a perianth; the two stamens have short filaments and the lobed stigma is pressed close to the globose ovary. Pepper plants with coloured leaves are also grown; for example *P. ornatum* with young leaves coloured carmine-red that later fade to greyish-pink, *P. porphyrophyllum* and *P. sylvaticum*.

P. nigrum may be placed in a light position, but it tolerates shade very well. The winter temperature should be about 15°C (59°F). The growing medium is usually a loam and peat compost. Water regularly to keep the compost permanently moist. The plant also benefits from misting. Feed weekly from spring to autumn. Propagate by stem and tip cuttings which require a temperature of about 25°C (77°F) for rooting. Always put several cuttings in one pot and cover them with a plastic bag, otherwise the plants will shed their leaves. All variegated species are more tender; in winter the temperature should not fall below 18°C (64°F).

Senecio-Cruentus —hybr.
Compositae

Cineraria (272, 273) is a hybrid of fairly uncertain parentage. One parent is thought to be *S. cruentus*, native to the Canary Islands. Nowadays, there are innumerable cultivars including

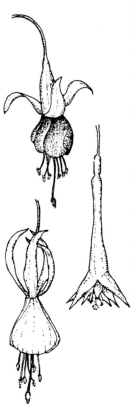

Fuchsia × *hybrida*
—flowers of various
cultivars

274

varieties with white, pink, blue or violet blooms, and even ones
with bicoloured flowers — red and white, blue and white, etc.
Interestingly, horticulturists have not succeeded in developing
a yellow-flowered Cineraria, even though yellow is a common
colour of other Senecio species. When the flowers are finished
the plant is discarded. In nurseries it is propagated every year
from seed. It is frequently planted outdoors in ceramic containers in parks and public gardens and is used as edging for
beds with other ornamental plants.

Because Cineraria originated in mountain forests with very
high humidity it requires a very moist atmosphere in the home;
moreover, the large leaves take up a lot of water. Besides regular watering, it is necessary to stand the pot in a bowl of water
so that the root ball does not dry out. Misting is inadvisable because it can damage the flowers. It requires light, but not direct
sunlight which makes the flowers fade.

283

275

Fuchsia × hybrida
Onagraceae

Fuchsias (274) are native to Central and South America, where they grow in forests up to elevations of 3,000 m (10,000 ft). A few species are found in New Zealand and Tahiti. They have been cultivated since the late 18th century. They are very rewarding plants, and their diverse flowers and the colour combinations of their sepals and petals are universally admired. There are about 100 different species and innumerable cultivars. The flowers have a long tube; the sepal colour is usually red and the petals are white. They range in size from very small to quite large. They may be simple, semi-double or double.

It grows well indoors in plenty of diffused light, but does not tolerate direct sunlight. In summer, it can be transferred outdoors to a garden or balcony. Water regularly and do not allow the compost to dry out, for then the leaves drop. Feed every two or three weeks during the growing period. Overwinter in a cool, light place at a temperature of 6°-10°C (43°-50°F). Water once every one to two months in winter. In February resume normal watering and repot the plants. To promote branching, pinch out the shoots. Propagate by tip cuttings, which will root within 10-20 days at a soil temperature of about 20°C (68°F).

Camellia japonica
Theaceae

Camellia (275). This is the only one of 80 species of Camellia grown as a house plant. It is native to Japan, Korea and China. This evergreen shrub or small tree is lovely even when not in flower. The leaves are ovate, leathery and very glossy with crenately-dentate margins. The large flowers – up to 12 cm (4³/₄ in) across — are usually solitary and sessile. The calyx is composed of five leathery sepals and the corolla of five to seven petals. There are a great many stamens. It is interesting to note that in the wild the flowers are pollinated by birds.

Cultivation is not difficult. The plant requires plenty of light and does best in the window in a cool room. However, it must be sheltered from direct sun and draughts and should be kept in the same position and not moved around. A suitable growing medium is a mixture of nourishing compost, peat and sand. The container must be provided with good drainage. In summer, it does well if moved to a partially shaded place in the garden. Water liberally in summer. In winter, maintain a temperature of 5°-10°C (41°-59°F); if the temperature rises above 15°C (59°F), the buds may fall prematurely. Water in winter according to the temperature — the lower the temperature, the less water the plant requires. It does not tolerate lime. Feed with organic fertilizer in April and May, and again in August. A compound fertilizer may also be used. Propagate by tip cuttings in a propagator at a soil temperature of 25°C (77°F) and at an ambient temperature of 20°-22°C (68°-72°F).

Hoya bella
Asclepiadaceae

Of the 100-200 species of wax flowers native to Asia and Australia only two, *H. carnosa* and *H. bella*, are grown indoors. *H. bella* (276) is smaller than *H. carnosa* and so does not need such frequent pruning. It is very well suited to a hanging container. The opposite leaves, only 25-30 mm (1-1¹/₅ in) long and 15-30 mm (¹/₂-1¹/₂ in) wide, are pointed-ovate and leathery. The sweetly scented flowers are 5-merous with a reddish corona.

It requires a light position but it should be sheltered from too much sun, which turns the leaves yellow. The growing medium must be nourishing and free-draining such as loam and peat compost with an addition of sand. It does well at normal room temperature; in winter the best temperature is about 18°C

278

(64°F). Water liberally during the growing period, from spring to autumn. In winter, water moderately; too much moisture causes the roots to rot. Propagate by stem cuttings, which need have no more than one pair of leaves. They will rapidly form roots at a temperature of about 20°-25°C (68°-77°F). Another reliable method is to graft this species on to *H. carnosa* root-stock in spring; the plants are then stronger and flower more profusely.

Hoya longifolia
Asclepiadaceae

This species (277), only rarely grown as a house plant, comes from the Himalayan foothills where it twines up trees in the forest. Like all other wax flowers, it has leathery, pointed leaves that are glossy in youth. It is readily identified by the flowers which open only slightly. It is smaller than the commonly cultivated *H. carnosa* and so is a particularly suitable plant for small houses and flats.

Conditions for growing are the same as for *H. bella* (see above). Ventilate the room regularly; wax flowers require plenty of fresh air. As they are lianas, growing them on an epiphyte stump is very successful; it comes closest to the way they grow in their natural habitat.

Tradescantia
fluminensis
'Albo-vittata'
Commelinaceae

This (278) is one of the commonest house plants. It is popular because it is easy to cultivate and to propagate by stem cuttings. Perhaps no other house plant lasts as long without compost, growing simply in water. *T. fluminensis* is very attractive in a hanging container. The stems are reddish and generally prostrate with ascending tips. The leaves are short-stalked, 2-4 cm (3/4-1 1/2 in) long and 15-20 mm (1/2-3/4 in) wide. Those of the illustrated cultivar are striped with white and some are nearly all white.

287

279

Hyacinthus orientalis
Liliaceae

Everybody will probably know hyacinths (279) whose lovely flowers gladden the heart and fill our homes with a heady fragrance in winter. They have been grown for decades since their introduction into cultivation from their native habitat in the eastern Mediterranean. It is a herb with a globose, violet-tinged bulb from which grow glossy, fleshy, linear-lanceolate leaves. These are 20-35 cm (8-14 in) long and 8-15 mm ($^3/_{10}$-$^1/_2$ in) wide, with a teardrop-shaped tip. The flower stem is stout and upright with a raceme of 5-20 flowers. The pendent flowers are relatively short-stalked and grow from the axils of three-sided bracts. The perianth is bell-like with recurved segments. The stamens do not protrude from the flowers.

To force a hyacinth so that it will flower in winter, plant the bulb in a pot filled with nourishing, free-draining compost, such as a heavy loam and peat substrate, in September or October. Keep it at a temperature of about 10°C (50°F) for approximately 11 weeks. When the leaves are about 5 cm (2 in) long put the pot in a dark place or cover it with a paper cone. Keep it like this for a week at a temperature of about 24°C (75°F). Then remove the cover, lower the temperature to normal room tem-

perature and the flowers will soon open. If you want the hyacinth to flower the following year as well, bring it to a dormant condition after it has finished flowering by limiting the supply of water. Store the bulb in a cool, dry place and in the autumn repeat the process of forcing. This time, however, the inflorescence will be much scantier. You can also plant the bulb out in the garden after the hyacinth has finished flowering indoors.

Cyclamen persicum
Primulaceae

tuber commencing growth

Cyclamen (280) is a short-term house plant; in other words one that is cultivated only during the flowering period. However, if it is provided with the proper conditions, it may even flower again. The genus Cyclamen has 14 species; *C. persicum* is native to Asia Minor.

It is important to provide flowering specimens with a low temperature of about 12°-15°C (54°-59°F) in winter; they will then produce flowers the whole winter. Equally important is ample light, but not direct sunlight. Water liberally in winter for otherwise the leaves as well as the flowers soon wilt. During the resting period from May to June water sparingly. Cyclamens are also good for cutting. If you want a long-lasting display, make several longitudinal cuts at the bottom of the stem.

282

**Clerodendrum
thomsoniae**
Verbenaceae

Glory Bower or Bleeding Heart Vine (281) is one of the very few lianas in this family. The genus Clerodendrum includes 450 species distributed in tropical and sub-tropical regions throughout the world. In its native home of West Africa it grows to a height of several metres, but there is no need to worry because the stems can be cut back without any problem. The red and white flowers are truly lovely. The calyces are inflated and composed of fine white sepals; the blood-red corolla with extremely narrow tube extends from these. The long green stamens and awl-shaped style protrude from the corolla.

This Clerodendrum does well in a light position with diffused light. It does not tolerate draughts and requires liberal watering. In winter, when the plant should be allowed a rest period of about two months, water sparingly and only when the soil has become dry. Ventilate the room frequently. The leaves drop during the resting period. Pruning is beneficial, especially as the flowers are produced only on the current year's wood. It is readily propagated in spring by means of tip cuttings. Put them in a mixture of peat and sand at a temperature of about 22°C (72°F). New plants should be potted up in heavier, nourishing compost, such as a mixture of frame soil and sand.

Clerodendrum
speciosissimum
Verbenaceae

This species (282) is native to Polynesia, the Sunda Islands and New Guinea. It is an upright shrub about 3 m (10 ft) high. The long-stalked, opposite leaves have prominent veins. They are tomentose on the upper surface and may even be white-felted on the underside. The flower panicles are large and borne at the tips of the branches. The calyx is purplish-red, the corolla scar-

284

let-red. The long filaments and style are also red. Growing conditions are the same as for *C. thomsoniae* (see above).

Clerodendrum ×
speciosum
Verbenaceae

This hybrid (283) is obtained from *C. splendens* and *C. thomsoniae*. It has pink sepals with a pointed apex and broadly obovate, scarlet-red petals. The filaments are red and white. Growing conditions are the same as for *C. thomsoniae* (see p. 291).

Eucharis grandiflora
Amaryllidaceae

Amazon Lily (284) is native to Colombia. Two to four bright green, parallel-veined leaves grow from the globose bulb, about 5 cm (2 in) across. They are more than 30 cm (12 in) long and

285

about 15 cm (6 in) wide. The lovely inflorescence is usually composed of three to six white blooms, 6-8 cm (2½-3 in) in diameter. The long, narrow tube, which may be straight or faintly curved, opens into six spreading lobes surrounding a white corona resembling a collar to which the stamens are attached.

A suitable growing medium is a mixture of leaf mould, rotted turves and sand. In summer it thrives at a temperature of 20°C (68°F). During the growing and flowering period it should be watered and misted liberally. Feed alternately with organic and compound fertilizers once a week. After the plant has finished flowering, limit watering for about a month. It may flower two to three times a year. Propagate by bulb offsets.

Rhoicissus rhomboides
(syn. *Cissus rhombifolia*)
Vitaceae

Plants of the Vitaceae family are rarely grown indoors. Those belonging to the genus Parthenocissus and Ampelopsis, for example, are definitely plants for outdoors. *R. rhomboides* (285) is native to Central and South America. It has a climbing stem with tendrils. However, these do not have adhesive pads as, for

example, those of Parthenocissus. The leaves are alternate, trifoliate and long-stalked. The leaflets are rhomboid, the central one larger than the two side leaflets, which are asymmetrical. The margin is dentate with a distinct vein extending from each tooth. The small, inconspicuous greenish flowers are arranged in umbels. The fruit is a one- to four-seeded berry. The plant's most decorative feature are the leaves.

If grown indoors, it does best in a light to partially shaded position. Water liberally and feed once a week with organic or inorganic fertilizers. It requires warm conditions throughout the year. Repot into nourishing compost every year. The plant should be propagated by stem cuttings (neither woody nor too soft) taken in summer.

Cissus striata
Vitaceae

This evergreen liana (286), native to Chile and southern Brazil, has hairy stems with branched tendrils and five-lobed leaves. The individual leaflets are leathery, wedge-shaped at the base and toothed on the margin.

It does best in rather cool conditions up to 18°C (64°F). Other requirements are the same as for *Rhoicissus rhomboides* (see above).

Haemanthus katharinae
Amaryllidaceae

Blood Lily (287), from South Africa, is the loveliest of the genus Haemanthus, which numbers some 60 species (distributed only in Africa). The most widely cultivated is *H. albiflos*, with yellowish-white flowers and leathery leaves growing to either side. *H. katharinae* is quite different. It has a large bulb from which grows a stout stem. The leaves are large, up to 30 cm (12 in) long, with prominent veins. The flowers, which appear at the same time as the leaves, are blood-red (hence the generic name) and arranged in dense, globose umbels up to 25 cm (10 in) in diameter. The individual flowers have narrow stalks, 3 cm (1 in) long, pointed perianth segments and very prominent stamens that extend far out from the flower. The cultivar 'König's Albert' is well known. It is more robust and has scarlet-red flowers. It was introduced to the market about 1900.

287

fruiting plant beginning to die back

288

It grows best in a miniature conservatory but also does well in a position further away from the window with sufficient diffused light. Feed regularly during the growing season. During the resting period, from October to March, some leaves drop. Limit watering during this time. Propagate either by bulb offsets or by seeds.

Sinningia × hybrida
Gesneriaceae

tuber commencing growth

The large, beautiful flowers make Gloxinia (288) one of the most popular house plants. The large, velvety leaves, wrinkled along the veins, are also attractive. The trumpet-like flowers, up to 5 cm (2 in) in length, have a long tube opening into five wavy lobes. The illustrated hybrid, descended from *S. speciosa*, has given rise to innumerable cultivars, differing mainly in the colour of the flowers. These are various combinations and shades of pink, red, violet and blue. There are also some with 'crinkly' flowers. This plant is commonly called Gloxinia, which is, in fact, the scientific name of a closely related genus.

It is usually grown only for short term decoration in the home, but the tubers may be lifted and overwintered in a cool, dry place and then replanted in nourishing compost in spring. A mixture of frame soil, leaf mould, peat, sand and charcoal is recommended. Feed regularly with organic fertilizer. Water liberally to keep the compost moist but do not allow the water to come into contact with the leaves because they rot quickly. Propagate by sowing seed on sterile peat. Alternatively, take whole leaves and insert the stalks in a mixture of sand and chopped peat in a propagator.

Monstera obliqua
Araceae

This Monstera (289) is a much rarer species than the commonly cultivated *M. deliciosa*. It is native to the forests of Brazil and the conditions for growing are the same as for all other Monsteras. It has long ovate leaves which are not lobed and incised, but entire on the margin and perforated on either side of the midrib; these perforations are usually ellipsoid. The leaf blade is 20-25 cm (8-10 in) long.

All Monsteras should be grown in a loam and peat compost. Water regularly but not too liberally; rather dry compost is tolerated better than soggy compost. Monsteras have no special humidity requirements. The ideal temperature for most species is 15°-20°C (59°-68°F), and even lower in winter. *M. obliqua*, however, requires greater warmth, about 20°C (68°F) in winter, and also more diffused light. Soilless cultivation in hydroponic containers is a recommended method. Propagate by tip and stem cuttings.

Syngonium podophyllum 'Albolineatum'
Araceae

Goose Foot (290) is an aroid native to the forests of Central America, where it climbs up tree trunks. The stems are covered with numerous aerial roots as well as alternate, long-stalked leaves. These are extremely variable: those of juvenile forms are completely different from the leaves of adult plants — sagittate at first, later divided into five to nine leaflets. The leaves of the

289

290

cultivar 'Albolineatum' have prominent, yellow or white markings. It is generally grown for its ornamental foliage, but the flowers, consisting of a spadix enclosed by a yellowish-white spathe, are also decorative. The fruit is a berry coloured deep red when ripe.

This is a rapidly-growing plant, particularly if it is provided with sufficient light. However, it also tolerates partial shade. When grown in full sun the colour of the leaves fades. It requires quite high humidity. The optimum temperature for growth is 20°C (68°F); in winter 18°C (64°F) is sufficient. Propagate by tip or stem cuttings, taken with at least two leaves. Other conditions are the same as for *Monstera obliqua* (see opposite page). It is very well suited for growing on an epiphyte stump, which it soon covers, or trained over a framework such as a room divider. It is also effective grown together with brightly flowered plants.

Vinca rosea
(syn. *Catharanthus roseus*)
Apocynaceae

Madagascar Periwinkle (291) is native to the region stretching from Madagascar to Indonesia. Like most members of the family, it is poisonous, but is an attractive and undemanding plant that flowers from June to October. It is a pity that it is so little grown in the household nowadays. One of the reasons, perhaps, is that growers erroneously believed it to be an annual and dis-

299

carded specimens that had finished flowering. The pink flowers, 25-35 mm (1-1⅖ in) across, with a velvety, carmine-red centre, are very decorative.

In summer, it is best to transfer the plant to a partially shaded position in the garden. At higher temperatures it should be watered liberally; at lower temperatures watering should be limited. Overwinter the plant at a temperature of about 15°C (59°F) and provide it with sufficient light. Prune early in spring and it will rapidly make new growth. Propagate by cuttings at a temperature above 20°C (68°F).

Crossandra infundibuliformis
Acanthaceae

This (292) is becoming increasingly popular as a house plant. The natural habitat of the 50 species that make up the genus is India and Sri Lanka. *C. infundibuliformis*, reaching a height of 30-50 cm (12-20 in) in cultivation, has both ornamental flowers and attractive foliage. The leaves are opposite, leathery and very glossy. The flowers, appearing from spring until autumn, are arranged in terminal spikes and grow from the axils of large green bracts.

It requires a light position, but not in direct sun. Water and mist regularly. A mixture of loam and peat is a good growing medium. Propagation from seed is not recommended. The best method is by tip cuttings taken in February and provided with a temperature of 20°-22°C (68°-72°F) for rooting. After they have rooted, the plants must be pruned so they will make bushy growth.

Graptophyllum pictum
Acanthaceae

This plant's (293) origins are not precisely known, but it is believed to be native to New Guinea and the neighbouring islands. It is widely distributed throughout the tropics, where it has been grown as an ornamental plant in gardens for decades. The generic name refers to the variegated leaves and is derived from Greek (*graptos* = painted, and *phyllom* = leaf). The leaves are 10-15 cm (4-6 in) long, elliptic, entire and purple or green with prominent, but irregular, yellow and white patches. The flowers, arranged in crowded clusters, measure about 3 cm (1 in). They are purple and have two lips, a typical characteristic of most members of the Acanthaceae family. The genus Graptophyllum is sometimes mistaken for the closely related genus Pseuderanthemum.

It does well in a light position but does not tolerate direct sunlight. It is more usually grown in a heated greenhouse than in the home. The temperature may be slightly higher than normal room temperature. The compost should contain ample peat

and be kept very moist. Propagate by dividing the clumps or by tip cuttings.

Tetrastigma
voinieranum
(syn. *Vitis voinierana*)
Vitaceae

This species (294) is a rare, evergreen liana, native to north Vietnam. It is usually grown in a greenhouse rather than in the home because it is so big. However, it may be kept within reasonable bounds by pruning. The leaves are long-stalked and five-lobed, composed of leathery leaflets up to 25 cm (10 in) long. They are coarsely toothed on the margin, glabrous above and brownish-felted on the underside. The generic name is derived from Greek (*tetra* = four, and *stigma*), and refers to the structure of the flowers. These are 4-merous and have a four-branched stigma, unlike the other members of the vine family, which have a cephaloid stigma.

Normal room temperature is sufficient. In winter, the plant will tolerate temperatures as low as 10°C (50°F). Water liberally in summer and moderately in winter. It should be grown in a nourishing compost. Feed with organic or compound fertilizer once a week. Protect from direct sun. Propagate by stem cuttings, taken with one leaf. These will root within three to four weeks at a soil temperature of about 25°C (77°F).

293

294

Pisonia umbellifera
(syn. *P. brunoniana,*
Heimerliodendron
brunonianum)
Nyctaginaceae

This plant (295) is native to New Zealand and to islands of the Pacific and Indian Oceans, where it grows to a height of 6 m (20 ft). There is no need to worry about its becoming too tall, for it can be easily pruned and kept to a reasonable size without any harm to the plant. It is grown for its ornamental foliage. The opposite leaves, up to 40 cm (16 in) long, are leathery and coloured dark green with prominent, yellowish or creamy-white patches. The inconspicuous greenish flowers are hardly ever produced by potted plants.

It requires a light position but it should be protected against direct sun. It thrives at high temperatures. Do not allow the temperature to fall below 18°C (64°F) in winter. A loam and peat

compost is best. Water regularly to keep the compost constantly moist. Feed the plants from spring to autumn with a stronger concentration of liquid fertilizer every one or two weeks. This is particularly important for plants that have not been repotted. Propagate by tip cuttings, which require a temperature of at least 25°C (77°F) to root.

Scutellaria costaricana
Labiatae

This plants (296) is native to Costa Rica, where it grows in the mountain forests at elevations as high as 2,000 m (6,500 ft). It is grown as a house plant for its lovely, glowing red flowers which are borne in rich terminal clusters. It is a member of the mint family, so it has a bilabiate corolla with two lips: the upper one is red and the lower one is yellow. The corolla tube is strikingly long. The opposite leaves are pointed ovate with toothed margins. The stem is quadrangular, another typical characteristic of plants of the mint family.

Because it is exposed to rugged conditions at night in its native habitat, it does not need very warm conditions in the home. Propagate by tip cuttings, when a higher temperature, about 22°C (72°F), is required. Young plants may be pruned to promote bushy growth, but this generally results in smaller inflorescences. As a rule, three to four plants are planted together in a single pot.

Schefflera actinophylla Queensland Umbrella Tree (297) reaches a height of 2 m (6½ ft)
Araliaceae when it is grown in a large container; in its native Australia, however, it grows to a height of 40 m (131 ft). The genus is named after the 18th-century Danish botanist J. C. Scheffler. There are approximately 150 species in the genus, distributed throughout the tropics. The striking leaves are composed of

296

305

297

7-15 long-stalked leaflets measuring up to 30 cm (12 in) in length. They are leathery, dark green and very glossy. Schefflera is grown only for its lovely foliage; it does not produce flowers indoors. In its native habitat, however, it bears red flowers arranged in umbels (the typical inflorescence of the Araliaceae family).

It does best in a light position, but should be sheltered from direct sun. It will also do well in partial shade. Normal room temperature is adequate for good growth; in winter, it requires a temperature of about 16°C (61°F) during the day and about 10°C (50°F) at night. Water liberally during the growing period. Propagate by non-woody tip cuttings. Mature plants can be propagated by air layering.

298

Dizygotheca elegantissima
(syn. *Aralia elegantissima*)
Araliaceae

False Aralia (298) is a woody plant with unusual foliage. Grown indoors it generally has a straight, unbranched stem. The leaves are long with very thin, green stalks with yellowish markings. The leaf blade is composed of seven to nine extremely narrow leaflets. They are olive-green with a reddish midrib and tip and prominently toothed on the margins. In cultivation it hardly ever produces flowers and fruits because house plants are usually juvenile plants. These are quite different from adult specimens, which can make identification of the individual species in the wild rather difficult. The precise number of species in the genus Dizygotheca is not known, but is estimated to be about 15. They are distributed in Polynesia and New Caledonia.

False Aralia is not very easy to cultivate. It requires a relative humidity of 50 per cent, but does not tolerate very wet compost. Always use tepid water for watering. It also does well in hydroponic cultivation. Propagate from seed or by grafting on to the related species *Meryta denhamii.*

299

**Ficus sagittata
'Variegata'**
(syn. *F. radicans*)
Moraceae

The genus Ficus includes an immense number of species — an estimated 2,000. They are therefore sub-divided into several groups according to whether they are evergreen or deciduous, and whether the stems are erect, climbing, or prostrate. *F. sagittata* (299), native to the Philippines, Micronesia and the eastern Himalayas, belongs to the last group. It has trailing stems that root at the nodes. The evergreen leaves are about 5 cm (2 in) long. They are longish lanceolate with a rounded base and completely glabrous. The leaves of the illustrated cultivar have creamy-white markings, some are practically completely white. Unlike the leaves of the similar *F. pumila,* the leaves of this species are symmetrical.

It is best grown in a plant case, but is also very attractive in a pot with its densely leaved stems trailing over the sides. When grown in a pot, it must be watered regularly so that the compost does not become dry; otherwise the leaves dry and shrivel. It does well in both warm and cool conditions. Propagate by tip cuttings. These root quickest in a propagator, hotbed, or, at least, under glass. Always put several young plants in one pot.

300

Ixora coccinea
Rubiaceae

Flame-of-the-woods (300) is rarely grown as an indoor plant. It reaches a height of about 1 m (39 in) in cultivation but in the forests of its native India it grows to a height of 5 m (16 ft). Ixora is a large genus — more thay 400 species have been described. They are to be found in all tropical regions but the majority grow in Asia. When not in flower, its leathery leaves are reminiscent of some citrus plants. The most spectacular feature is the globose flower clusters, almost 10 cm (4 in) across and coloured scarlet. The 4-merous calyces of the individual

301

flowers are small, but the corolla with an extremely narrow tube opening into four widespreading petals is a striking feature. A great advantage of this species is that flowers are produced even by small plants.

It requires plenty of diffused light but it must be sheltered from direct sun. In summer, it requires a temperature of about 18°-20°C (64°-68°F). The minimum winter temperature is 14°C (57°F). Water liberally and feed once a week during the growing season. Restrict watering in winter and for four weeks after flowering. It requires quite high humidity. The plants must be pruned to promote bushy growth. Propagate by tip cuttings. They root best in a propagator at a temperature of 25°-30°C (77°-95°F).

Furcraea selloa
'Marginata'
Agavaceae

This plant (301) is native to Colombia and resembles a dracaena or agave in its habit of growth. It owes its generic name to the French chemist A. T. Fourcroy. The genus includes 25 species, all of which are distributed in the warmer regions of Central and South America and on some islands such as Cuba. The stem, up to 1 m (39 in) high, is thickly covered with lance-shaped leaves. These are 7-10 cm (2¾-4 in) wide, dark green, very rough on the surface and spiny-toothed on the margins. The brown spines are distant and hooked. The inflorescence, usually quite tall, is composed of flowers about 6 cm (2½ in) long with greenish bracts. It is not often seen indoors, even though it is not an unduly demanding plant. It is sensitive, however, to low temperatures.

302

Ledebouria socialis
—tillering

Ledebouria socialis
(syn. *Scilla violacea*)
Liliaceae

Silver Squill (302) is native to Africa. Its bulb grows above the ground. Fleshy, narrow leaves with pointed tips grow from it. These are pale grey with prominent green, irregular, horizontal streaks on the upper surface, and glossy purple on the underside. In summer it produces panicles of 10-25 greenish flowers with violet stamens.

303

It is an undemanding plant, which grows well in a free-draining compost rich in humus. It does well at room temperature.
Water and mist fairly liberally. Feed with compound fertilizer
once every other month. Propagate by means of the many bulb
offsets.

305

Cordyline fruticosa 'Norwoodiensis'
Agavaceae

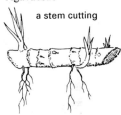

a stem cutting

Cordylines (303) are very close relatives of Dracaenas. They have the same strap-shaped or lanceolate leaves on a slender stem. Unlike Dracaenas, they have tuberous white roots. *C. fruticosa* is grown for its long-stalked leaves, measuring up to 50 cm (20 in) in length and striped reddish-brown.

Because this is a heat-loving species, it also requires quite high humidity. Mist or sponge the leaves regularly. The compost should never be allowed to dry out, but soggy compost is not tolerated either. There are no special light requirements. Propagate by tip, stem or root cuttings.

Asclepias curassavica
Asclepiadaceae

Blood Flower (304) is an upright sub-shrub native to tropical America. It is rarely seen in cultivation. It reaches a height of 50-70 cm (20-28 in). The leaves are opposite, short-stalked and 8-12 cm (3-4¾ in) long. They are dark green on the upper surface and blue-green on the underside. The lovely flower clusters are usually composed of ten flowers. Each has five widespreading scarlet petals. These form a vivid contrast to the orange corona, which is composed of five cupped segments with pointed tips extending towards the centre of the flower. These extraordinary blossoms open in late summer, usually in August but also in September.

Store the plant in a cool place, about 10°C (50°F), in winter to force early flowers in May or June. However, they will not be as decorative as the summer flowers. Propagate from seed sown any time from January to March. Plant three to five young plants in a pot about 17 cm (7 in) in diameter.

Dichorisandra reginae
Commelinaceae

Dichorisandra (305) is another genus of the Commelinaceae family, which also includes Tradescantia, Zebrina and Setcreasea. Dichorisandra includes about 30 species distributed throughout tropical South America. These have given rise to numerous cultivars. *D. reginae* is a herbaceous perennial with fleshy stem and alternate, variegated leaves with broad white stripes running parallel to the margins from base to leaf tip. The inflorescence is upright and composed of blue flowers with free sepals. The seeds have a large fleshy appendage, called an aril.

Conditions for growing are the same as for Tradescantia (see p. 339). Propagation is very easy. The commonest method is by stem cuttings which can either be inserted directly into compost or else put in water to root.

306

**Pleomele reflexa
'Variegata'**
(syn. *Dracaena reflexa*)
Agavaceae

This (306) lovely tropical plant closely resembles Dracaenas, among which it was originally classified. Its stems are thickly covered with long, narrow, faintly arching leaves. Those of the cultivar 'Variegata' are exceptionally decorative as they are edged with broad creamy to golden-yellow bands. Its rate of growth is slow, so it is unlikely to grow too tall and will not need to be pruned.

It does well in diffused light and tolerates even slight partial shade. The temperature in winter should be 18°-25°C (64°-77°F). In summer it will benefit by being transferred to the garden or a balcony. *P. reflexa* also does well in soilless cultivation. It is readily propagated by means of tip as well as stem cuttings, which rapidly form roots.

Jacobinia carnea
(syn. *Justicia carnea*)
Acanthaceae

The genus Jacobinia (307) includes about 40 species with some of the loveliest flowers of the Acanthaceae family. *J. carnea* is native to Brazil. The flowers are a delicate pink and arranged in crowded terminal clusters up to 8-10 cm (3-4 in) long. The corolla tube is narrow, expanding upwards and terminated by two

307

308

slightly downcurved lips. The large leaves, 20 cm (8 in) long, are opposite and hairy on both sides.

A rather high temperature is required. About 25°C (77°F) is a suitable temperature in summer and 16°-18°C (61°-64°F) is sufficient in winter. Light is also important; in a position with insufficient light, it grows too tall and loses its bushy habit. It needs a nourishing compost which should be kept permanently moist, even in winter. Feed with compound fertilizer once a week. Propagate by tip cuttings, taken in February or March and left in water to put out roots.

Dracaena marginata
Agavaceae

Madagascar Dragon Tree (308) is one of 40 species of Dracaena. Most are tropical plants of the Old World; only one (*D. americana*) is native to the New World. They have been grown for ornament for more than 100 years, first of all in greenhouses, later indoors. They are also highly prized in today's centrally-heated houses, for their decorative evergreen foliage. *D. marginata*, native to Madagascar, has a slender stem which grows to a height of 5 m (16 ft) in a greenhouse but is much shorter in indoor cultivation. It is white and marked with dark scars left by fallen leaves. The narrow, lanceolate leaves, embracing the stem with their base, are about 40 cm (16 in) long and only 2 cm ($^3/_4$ in) wide. They are fairly tough, upright, and dark green with brownish-red margins.

It requires quite a high temperature, a well ventilated location and plenty of diffused light. The compost should be kept constantly wet. Sponge the leaves frequently. Propagate by tip or stem cuttings, or by seed. Cuttings require a temperature of about 25°C (77°F) for rooting and seeds require the same temperature for germination.

Dracaena deremensis
Agavaceae

The type is cultivated only rarely, but its cultivars (309, 310) are very popular. The upright stems are thickly covered with narrowly lanceolate leaves up to 50 cm (20 in) long and 5 cm (2 in) wide. If left unpruned, the plants can grow to a height of 5 m (16 ft). The leaves of the type are green; those of the cultivars 'Bausei' (309) and 'Lemon Strip' (310) are striped.

309   310

311

Both cultivars require a light position, protected from direct sunlight. They are quite sensitive to temperature; the optimum temperature being 20°C (68°F). They grow well in hydroponic cultivation. The cultivation of pot-grown plants is the same as for *D. marginata* (see above).

Dracaena sanderiana
Agavaceae

This species (311) is of typical, slender, low-growing habit. It has curved, broadly lanceolate leaves, only 15-25 cm (6-8 in) long and 1-3 cm (^{2}/5-1 in) wide. They are striped green and silver.

This Dracaena has quite demanding heat and humidity requirements. Other cultivation requirements are the same as for *D. marginata* (see opposite page).

319

UNDEMANDING PLANTS

The main factors affecting the growth of plants are light, water, heat and compost. Plants that have no special requirements within these factors and that tolerate fluctuations in their growing conditions belong to the group of undemanding plants. In their natural habitat, their requirements differ from the conditions provided in the home, but they are capable of a certain amount of adaptation or, at least, are able to tolerate the changed conditions.

The least demanding plants are often cultivars accustomed to growing in cultivation. They are also frequently plants whose ecological variability is so great that they will tolerate numerous mistakes on the part of growers without any visible adverse effects on their beauty and vitality.

All plants the world over have some sort of annual cycle. Nowhere on earth is the temperature and the amount of rainfall the same throughout the year. Conditions in the home are regulated by Man to suit himself first, and not to suit the requirements of plants. Sometimes, he creates conditions to which the plants are unaccustomed at a time when they have the least need of them. The main difference between plants and Man is in their separate humidity requirements. The dry heat of modern, centrally-heated houses does not suit most plants, although it pleases people. As a result, plants requiring overwintering in cool conditions are disappearing from the scene, whereas species that tolerate a warm and dry environment are becoming increasingly popular.

Plants are sometimes left without water during holidays and they must often tolerate cold when the heating is switched off at night. Sometimes they are exposed to a stream of freezing air in a room that is usually overheated, while it is being aired. Fortunately, the light and compost conditions provided by the grower are generally well tolerated by undemanding plants.

313

314

Hedera helix
Araliaceae

leaves of various cultivars

In the wild, ivy (312, 313) grows in the undergrowth of shady woods or as an escape from gardens and cemeteries where it is commonly grown. It is also grown indoors as a decorative plant in hanging containers and bowls. Its evergreen foliage, the leaves exhibiting marked variability in shape as well as coloration, make it a popular house plant. Ivy is a climbing plant with numerous clinging rootlets with which it holds fast to trees, rocks and walls. It is heterophyllous, that is it has two kinds of leaves. Those on the sterile branches are an entirely different shape from those on the fertile (flowering) branches. The former are lobed, usually with three to five lobes, whereas the latter are ovate with an entire, unlobed margin. The inconspicuous yellow-green flowers are in small umbels and are produced only by older plants. The type is not suited for indoor cultivation because its growth is too vigorous and the rootlets cling to walls and furniture where they often cause damage. Most people prefer cultivars.

It tolerates shade well but will produce flowers only in a light position. It grows best in a compost containing lime. Ivy can be propagated throughout the year by stem cuttings. Cultivars with variegated foliage require a higher temperature for rooting. It

322

used to be grown mainly in cold rooms that were often shady as well. Nowadays, with so many cultivated forms which have higher temperature requirements, it is becoming a common ornamental plant even in modern centrally-heated houses. The most popular cultivated varieties are 'Argenteovariegata' with white markings on the leaves (312), 'Crispa' with curly edged leaves, 'Aureo-variegata' with yellowish markings, 'Ovata' with almost unlobed leaves, and 'Gloire de Marengo' with fairly large three-lobed, creamy-yellow leaves (313).

315

Aspidistra elatior
—the flower

Hoya carnosa
Asclepiadaceae

Wax Flower (314) is one of 200 Hoya species distributed throughout China, India and Australia. It may form woody stems up to several metres long. The leaves are opposite, stiff, leathery and glossy. The flowers are the most striking part of the plant and gave the plant its name. They look as if they were made of white or faintly pink wax. They have a very strong fragrance, particularly towards evening, which some people find overpowering. They also secrete a sticky fluid (nectar) that makes the area around the plant rather messy.

Wax Flower grows very rapidly and so must occasionally be pruned. It likes a light position but direct sunlight causes the leaves to turn yellow. In winter, limit watering; a temperature of 12°-15°C (54°-59°F) is the most suitable. Water liberally during the growing period. Other cultivation details are the same as given for *H. bella* (see p. 286).

Aspidistra elatior
Liliaceae

Bar-room Plant, Cannon-Ball Plant, Cast Iron Plant (315) — few house plants are as hardy and undemanding as this one, which tolerates a smoke-filled atmosphere, dry air and dust. Because it is native to the shady forests of Japan, it grows well even in poor light in a room or hall, but does not tolerate full sun. This evergreen is grown for its large leaves. The flowers are insignificant and easily overlooked, for they grow close to the ground and their colour makes them hard to distinguish. The eight perianth segments are interesting, as plants of the Lily family usually have 3-merous flowers. There are also eight stamens.

316

317

During the growing period, water the plant moderately, only when the compost is dry. Severely restrict watering in winter. It will tolerate a winter temperature as low as 2°C (36°F). It does not tolerate frequent repotting and so should be left in the same container for several years. When repotting, it is best to pot it up in a heavy loam and peat compost. Propagate by dividing the clumps when repotting. Each newly detached plant should have at least two leaves.

Zebrina pendula
(syn. *Tradescantia zebrina*)
Commelinaceae

This species (316) is native to Mexico and is now widely grown everywhere in houses as well as public buildings. Its popularity arises from its attractive appearance and its ability to propagate rapidly by cuttings which last several years just in water (with an occasional application of feed). The genus Zebrina includes four species formerly classed in the genus Tradescantia. The joined sepals and joined petals are typical of Zebrinas. The leaves are the most striking feature of *Z. pendula*. They have prominent silvery-white stripes on the upper surface and are red on the underside. They have a membranous sheath where they are attached to the stem. The stems are prominently geniculate and often red. The petals of the 3-merous flowers are pink inside and white outside.

318

It is often grown in glass containers of various sorts, such as
test tubes. If you want to grow it in a pot, always put several cuttings in the compost. These will rapidly form roots if watered
frequently. Older plants should not be repotted but renewed by
taking pieces of the plant and rooting them to grow into new

319

320

plants. Zebrina does best in diffused light; the colour of the leaves fades in sunlight. During the winter it tolerates temperatures as low as 6°C (43°F).

Setcreasea pallida
'Purple Heart'
(syn. *S. purpurea*)
Commelinaceae

The Commelinaceae family includes several genera with similar habits of growth. Delimiting the genera is by no means simple and botanists often differ in their opinions. Setcreasa (317) is most closely related to Zebrina, from which it differs by having unjoined sepals and petals joined only at the base. All parts of the plant are purple. The narrow leaves may be up to 20 cm (8 in) long and only 3-4 cm (1-1½ in) wide. The inflorescence is scanty. The flowers, measuring about 15-20 mm (³/₅-³/₄ in), are

327

pale purple and enclosed by two bracts. The type is native to Mexico. Its striking colour makes this an outstanding plant for room decoration. Conditions for growing are the same as for Zebrina and Tradescentia (see p. 325 and p. 339).

Fatsia japonica
(syn. *Aralia japonica*)
Araliaceae

The genus Fatsia (318) includes only this species. As the specific name indicates, it is native to Japan, where it grows as a shrub to a height of 5 m (16 ft). The long-stalked leaves are evergreen, leathery and with seven to nine lobes. They are glossy on the upper surface, dull on the underside, and generally broader than they are long — they can be up to 40 cm (16 in) wide. The flowers are fairly inconspicuous. They are white, arranged in small umbels, and usually appear from July to September. Fatsia is greatly valued as an ornamental plant, growing by itself or with other plants. Very large and old specimens are used to decorate foyers, concert halls and hallways. In summer they are also put outdoors in large ceramic pots in public areas.

Fatsia thrives in a rather cool and light location. It requires a nourishing compost, such as a loam and peat mixture. Water regularly. At high temperatures it becomes unattractive. The best temperature for overwintering is 4°-8°C (39°-46°F). In

321

summer it does very well in the garden or on a shaded bacony or patio. It will also grow well in soilless cultivation. Plants that have become leggy and too tall may be rejuvenated by being cut back hard, but first let the top form roots directly on the plant by air layering.

Ophiopogon jaburan
Liliaceae

Lily Turf (319) can be recommended for those who require an undemanding plant for a shady position. It can be grown in a pot or as a ground cover in a conservatory, for example. It forms attractive clumps of narrow, grass-like leaves, about 40-70 cm (16-28 in) long, 5-15 mm ($\frac{1}{5}$-$\frac{1}{2}$ in) wide. They are fairly stiff and dark green. The cultivar 'Variegatus' (319), with striped golden-yellow leaves, is also popular. The flowers are white, small, about 1 cm ($\frac{2}{5}$ in), and arranged in crowded spikes. The flower spikes are usually hidden by the leaves, very occasionally rising above them.

Conditions for growing this plant are the same as for *Acorus gramineus* (see p. 213). It does best in cool conditions. The compost should be kept constantly moist. It is readily propagated by dividing the clumps.

323

Ruellia portellae
(syn. *Dipteracanthus portellae*)
Acanthaceae

The genus includes 200-250 species, all distributed throughout the tropics. *R. portellae* (320), native to Brazil, is a low-growing, prostrate plant with only some of its shoots reaching a height of 30 cm (12 in). It is very branched so that it rapidly fills the planting position. The leaves are longish ovate with a pointed tip, 5-7 cm (2-2³/₄ in) long and 3-4 cm (1-1¹/₂ in) wide. A broad

324

white to yellow stripe runs along the midrib and narrower stripes run along the secondary veins. The leaves are pinkish-red on the underside. The flowers, which do not appear until late autumn or the beginning of winter, grow singly from the axils of the leaves and are coloured pink.

This rewarding plant does well in shade and therefore can be planted beneath taller plants. It also looks very attractive in a shallow dish. It requires plenty of warmth. In winter, the temperature may fall as low as 15°C (59°F). Water regularly. A good compost is a mixture of two parts leaf mould, one part peat and half a part sand. Propagate by tip cuttings or seed.

Chamaeranthemum beyrichii
Acanthaceae

This species (321) is becoming a popular house plant not only because of its variegated foliage, but also for its low-growing habit. The genus Chamaeranthemum has only four species, found in tropical South America. *C. beyrichii* is from southern Brazil. It grows to a maximum height of 10 cm (4 in). The leaves are large, opposite, ovate, stiff and glabrous. During the flowering period, upright clusters of small, white flowers subtended by minute bracts protrude above the leaves.

325

Because this is a low-growing plant with greater moisture requirements, it used to be grown in a plant case but it is now known that it does equally well in normal room conditions. Normal room temperature is sufficient for good growth, but a higher temperature is very beneficial. Water liberally. A good growing medium is a loam and peat compost. Three to five young plants are usually planted together. If it has enough space it rapidly spreads not only by vegetative means, but also by means of seeds which are ejected by the plant itself.

Philodendron wendlandii
Araceae

Philodendron is a genus that is very closely related to Monstera. It includes some 200 species distributed throughout tropical America. *P. wendlandii* (322) is native to Costa Rica and Panama. Philodendrons are either lianas or woody plants with upright stems that may grow to a huge size. They often form aerial roots up to several metres in length. *P. wendlandii* has very stiff, leathery, prominently ribbed leaves that form a huge rosette. The wing-like leaf stalks are striking. The flower spadix is creamy-yellow.

It requires peaty compost with an addition of sand and frame soil or leaf mould. Water regularly to keep the compost moist but not soggy; it does not matter if it dries out occasionally. Normal room temperature is suitable for good growth; in winter it may fall to 16°C (61°F). Propagate by cuttings which require a temperature of 25°C (77°F) for rooting. All species of Philodendron have the same cultivation requirements. Provide a moss pole for climbing types.

Philodendron
verrucosum
Araceae

This species (323) is native to the forests of Costa Rica and Colombia. The most conspicuous features are the leaf stalks which are up to 50 cm (20 in) long and thickly covered with hairs. The

heart-shaped leaf is dark green flushed with brown along the veins and emerald green along the margins.

It requires a higher temperature and liberal watering. It has the same cultivation requirements as *P. verrucosum* (see above).

Philodendron elegans
Araceae

This species (324) typically has heart-shaped leaves with very narrow, linear segments, up to 70 cm (28 in) in length and 50 cm (20 in) in width. It grows in the tropical forests of South America as a liana that climbs high in the treetops. There is no need to worry about its growing too high indoors because it can be kept to a reasonable size by pruning. The cuttings can be used to grow new plants; they root well just in water. It has the same cultivation requirements as *P. verrucosum* (see above).

Philodendron scandens
Araceae

This Philodendron (325), native to the Antilles, differs from the preceding species by having extremely thin stems which may be as much as several metres long and are covered with small, heart-shaped leaves. The leaf blade is only 8-14 cm (3-5½ in) long and 5-9 cm (2-3½ in) wide and glossy on the upper side.

It does well in a light position and even in partial shade. It should be protected from direct sunlight, which causes the leaves to fade and turn yellow. It is a very good plant for soilless cultivation in a hydroponic container and looks attractive placed on a shelf from which its stems trail downwards. It is also often planted beside a moss pillar. It has rather demanding moisture requirements.

329

Philodendron selloum
Araceae

This species (326) is native to Brazil and Paraguay. It has been grown in cultivation since 1850. It has magnificent foliage with deeply lobed leaf blades up to 50 cm (20 in) long and 70 cm (28 in) wide. The lobes are wavy on the margin. Conditions for growing are the same as for *P. scandens* (see the opposite page).

Monstera deliciosa
Araceae

Swiss Cheese Plant (327, 328) is native to Mexico. It is rightly considered to be indestructible. Its leaves are incised, but the perforations appear only on mature plants. The leaves of young specimens are entire. Only when four or five leaves have developed do the perforations begin to form in the oldest leaf.

The ideal temperature throughout most of the year is 21°C (70°F), but, in winter, even a fall to 16°C (61°F) or as low as 12°C (54°F) will cause no harm. A mixture of peat and loam is generally used as the growing medium. Water liberally. A light position is best. The leaves of specimens grown in dark places

335

are usually without perforations. Propagation is by means of cut-up pieces of the stem, which may even be without a leaf. They will root in a propagator or just in water.

Epipremum aureum
(syn. *Pothos aureus*)
Raphidophora aurea,
Scindapsus aureus)
Araceae

Ivy Arum (329, 330) is one of the commonest house plants. This liana is native to the Solomon Islands where it climbs to great heights on all sorts of trees. This characteristic can be put to good use indoors where it can be trained over walls or various kinds of netting and frames, even quite far from the window.

It does well in a light position and in partial shade, but does not tolerate direct sunlight. Water regularly throughout the year. It also does very well in hydroponic cultivation. Propagation is very easy. Simply insert stem cuttings in water where they will rapidly form roots.

The leaves of *E. aureum* (329) are heart-shaped with streaks of yellow. Horticulturists have developed many cultivars with coloured leaves. The cultivar 'Erich Gedalinus' (330) (syn. 'Marble Queen') is interesting in that the markings are white, whereas in other cultivars they are usually yellow. It is more demanding and so harder to grow. The temperature should not fall below 15°C (59°F) and it should also be provided with a more humid atmosphere. It is very attractive tied to a moss pillar. This is moisture-retentive and so is very beneficial to the plants that twine around it for support. The stems can also be allowed to trail downwards instead of being trained up a frame.

Aucuba japonica
Cornaceae

This evergreen, dioecious shrub (331), native to the sub-tropical forests of Japan and southern Korea, reaches a height of 2 m (6½ ft). The opposite leaves are 6-20 cm (2½-8 in) long, pointed, irregularly toothed, and glossy. The 4-merous flowers are small, red, and arranged in short panicles. The red fruits (drupes) are small, about 1 cm (⅖ in). There are numerous cultivars differing chiefly in the markings on the leaves and in their consistency.

331

'Crassifolia', for example, has very stiff, leathery leaves; a distinguishing feature of 'Luteocarpa' is its yellow fruit.

It is an absolutely undemanding plant, grown both as a potted plant and in parks and gardens. In Europe, it requires a sheltered situation outdoors but, even if slightly damaged by frost, it makes vigorous new growth in spring. This can be cut back and the cuttings inserted in the soil to root. It requires cool conditions for good growth.

334

Chlorophytum
comosum
Liliaceae

vegetative propagation

Spider Plant (332, 333) is native to South Africa and has been cultivated since the mid-19th century. It has extremely thick, yellow roots. Its leaves are arranged in a fairly large, dense rosette. The type has green foliage, but it is rarely grown as a house plant. Far commoner are the cultivars with leaves striped white or yellow such as 'Milky Way' (332), or variegated forms, listed collectively as 'Variegatum' cultivars (333). The leaves are narrow, 40 cm (16 in) long, 25 mm (1 in) wide and usually arching. A long flower stem, terminated by small, white, 3-merous flowers grows from the centre of the leaf rosette. Numerous plantlets with roots also form on the stems. When they are severed from the parent plant, they may be inserted immediately in compost and grown in pots.

It will last many years indoors but does not produce flowers regularly. It requires a light situation but should be protected from direct sunlight which causes the leaves to fade. Water regularly. It grows well at normal room temperature. It can be repotted any time of the year. A suitable growing medium is a mixture of frame soil, rotted turves, peat and sand. It is grown not only in pots but also in hanging containers and, in summer, is often planted in outdoor beds with decorative annuals.

Tradescantia albiflora
Commelinaceae

This species (334) has green stems and leaves, and white flowers, but these are only rarely produced. It is grown mainly for its decorative foliage.

It does best in diffused light and does not tolerate full sun or deep shade. It is a good plant for hydroponic cultivation.

339

Propagate by stem cuttings inserted either into water or directly into compost, about ten to a pot.

Spathiphyllum wallisii
Araceae

White Sails, Lily of Peace (335) is a very rewarding plant of the Arum family. The genus Spathiphyllum includes about 30 species growing primarily in tropical America; two are native to Asia. Lily of Peace bears flowers in succession from spring to autumn, making it an attractive addition to a room for a long time. It is a perennial herb with a very short stem from which rises a rosette of large leaves. The leaf stalks and leaf blades reach a length of about 25 cm (10 in). However, the leaves are only 4-7 cm (1½-2¾ in) wide. The dark leaf blade is longish lanceolate with a long point. The flowers are borne on long stems that extend beyond the leaves. The spadix is yellow; the spathe is white and extremely narrow, 3 cm (1 in) wide and 7 cm (2¾ in) long.

Cultivation is very simple for it is an undemanding plant that will grow even in the shade. Normal room temperature is quite suitable. Water liberally. Propagate by dividing the clumps. Because Spathiphyllum can grow submersed in water, it is also planted in aquariums.

335

submersed form

336

**Begonia-Corallina
—hybr.
'Luzerna'**
Begoniaceae

This hybrid's (336) origin is not definitely known. It was developed in the early 19th century, probably by crossing either
B. corallina and *B. c.* 'Madame Charrat', or *B. corallina* and
B. teuscheri. Some Begonias are grown for the ornamental foliage, others for their decorative flowers. This hybrid has both. It
may reach a height of 2 m (6½ ft) but is readily kept to a reasonable size by pruning; the tip cuttings may be used for propagation. The leaves are conspicuously asymmetrical. They may be
up to 35 cm (14 in) long and 9-15 cm (3½-6 in) wide. The large,
drooping inflorescences are pink or red.

It is considered to be the hardiest of the Begonias and so the
best suited for indoor cultivation. It requires a light position but

341

337

should be sheltered from direct sunlight, at least in summer. Normal room temperature is quite suitable, but the winter temperature should not fall below 18°C (64°F). It requires an acid compost. A suitable growing medium is a mixture of peat, sand and compost. Water liberally and feed every one or two weeks.

Cissus antarctica
Vitaceae

Kangaroo Vine (337) is perhaps the most widely cultivated of the 300 species of the large genus Cissus. It is native to Australia where it grows in damp forests. This evergreen liana becomes woody in time. The stems and leaf stalks are covered with short, rusty-brown hairs. The leaves, 10-12 cm (4-4¾ in) long and 8 cm (3 in) wide, are almost heart-shaped in outline, long-pointed and sharply toothed on the margins. They are glabrous, except along the veins on the underside, which are glandular-hairy. The flowers are quite inconspicuous; the plant is grown only for its foliage.

It is extremely undemanding, but does not tolerate high temperatures or a dry atmosphere. It does well even in partial shade. Transfer it to a cool place in winter. Feed with either organic or inorganic fertilizer about once a week. Repot young plants every spring; older plants every two to three years. Propagate by cuttings, which soon form roots if the pot is covered with a glass jar.

SUGGESTIONS FOR FURTHER READING

Böhmig F.: *Topfpflanzen.* — Neumann Verl., Radebeul 1958

Encke F. (red.): *Pareys Blumengärtnerei.* I-II. Ed. 2. – Parey, Berlin-Hamburg 1958—1960

Encke F. et al.: *Zander's Handwörterbuch der Pflanzennamen.* Ed. 2. — Ulmer Verl., Stuttgart 1979

Encke F.: *Kübelpflanzen.* Geschichte, Herkunft, Pflege.—Ulmer Verl., Stuttgart 1982

Fast. G. (red.): *Orchideenkultur.*—Ulmer Verl., Stuttgart 1980

Graf A. B.: *Pictorial Encyclopedia of Exotic Plants from Tropical and Near-Tropic Regions.* Ed. 9, revised. (Exotica ser. 3.) — Roehrs Company inc., E. Rutheford 1978

Haustein E.: *Der Kosmos-Kakteenführer.*—Franckh Verl., Stuttgart 1983

Jacobsen H.: *Das Sukkulentenlexikon.* Ed. 2.—Fischer Verl., Jena 1981

Lamb E. and Lamb B.: *Popular Exotic Cacti in Colour.*—Blandford Press Ltd., London 1975

Rauh W.: *Bromelien.* Ed. 2.—Ulmer Verl., Stuttgart 1981

Rauh W.: *Schöne Kakteen und andere Sukkulenten.* Ed. 2. — Borntraeger, Berlin-Stuttgart 1978

Richter W.: *Orchideen pflegen—vermehren—züchten.* Ed. 2.—Neumann Verl., Radebeul 1971

Rücker K.: *Die Pflanzen im Haus.*—Ulmer Verl., Stuttgart 1982

Squire D. and McHoy P. (red.): *The Book of Houseplants.*—Octopus Books Limited, London 1978

Šubík R.–Kaplická J.: *Cacti and Succulents.*–Aventinum, Prague 1969

INDEX

345